OTHER BOOKS FROM
THE EMILY POST INSTITUTE:

Emily Post's Etiquette,
16th Edition

Emily Post's Weddings,
Third Edition

Emily Post's Wedding Planner,
Third Edition

Emily Post's Entertaining

ALSO IN THE EMILY POST'S
ESSENTIALS SERIES:

Everyday Etiquette

Published by HarperPaperbacks

ESSENTIALS

EASY
ENTERTAINING

PEGGY POST

HarperPaperbacks
A Division of HarperCollinsPublishers

HarperPaperbacks
A Division of HarperCollins*Publishers*
10 East 53rd Street, New York, NY 10022-5299

For information address HarperCollins Publishers Inc., 10 East 53rd Street, New York, NY 10022–5299.

ISBN 0-06-273664-7

HarperCollins®, ◼®, and HarperPaperbacks™ are trademarks of HarperCollins Publishers Inc.

First HarperPaperbacks printing: July 1999

Printed in the United States of America

Visit HarperPaperbacks on the World Wide Web at
http://www.harpercollins.com

◆ 10 9 8 7 6 5 4 3 2 1

CONTENTS

INTRODUCTION

Entertaining others can be a daunting proposition to many hosts and hostesses. I hear from many people that they feel mired in minute details or constrained by antiquated formalities. But over the years, I've discovered the real truth about entertaining: Creating a fine occasion doesn't have to be complicated or stressful. If you have the answers to basic questions—such as how to make guests feel welcome or how to set a table—you'll discover that the etiquette of entertaining is really all about using applying consideration and common sense. Indeed, as a seasoned guest and host of all manner of celebrations, my great-grandmother-in-law Emily Post didn't blink if a fork was misplaced or a wineglass was the wrong size; that's because she felt that making guests feel comfortable and welcome was the host's top priority. The real reason for hosting a special occasion, after all, has less to do with displaying the good silver or impressing guests with a fancy formal meal than with making sure that guests are enjoying one another and the occasion.

My purpose in writing *Emily Post's Essentials: Easy Entertaining* is to demystify party-giving and take the stress out of entertaining. To that end, this book contains straightforward, practical tips on hosting both large parties and small—tips guaranteed to answer any questions you may have about the etiquette of entertaining. As a quick reference tool, *Easy Entertaining* will prove invaluable—you'll be delighted to find it's also a lively, informative read. I've included some of my most-requested entertaining tips, such as:

- The time frame for mailing invitations to different events
- Gift ideas for guests who want to give something to a host
- What hosting a baby shower entails
- How to make a toast
- How to eat unfamiliar or hard-to-manage foods
- Who stands in a receiving line
- How to host a business lunch
- How to work with a caterer
- Last-minute entertaining

Whether you're celebrating casually with a handful of friends or hosting a large formal reception, you can use this at-a-glance guide to help you adapt or tailor plans to meet new or changing situations, as the occasion dictates. As you celebrate the milestone occasions in your life, *Easy Entertaining* is certain to become as dog-eared and familiar as your favorite cookbooks. I think of it as a practical primer on hosting any celebration. Let *Easy Entertaining* give you the confidence and know-how to fully participate in the joyous times of your life.

—Peggy Post
March 1999

Emily Post's
ESSENTIALS

EASY ENTERTAINING

PART I

PREPARING FOR A FINE OCCASION

How does a good host or hostess ensure that a good time is had by all? Entertaining is a joy when you keep the following in mind.

REMAIN CALM. Entertaining doesn't have to be a monumental chore, taking on the proportions of a crisis; simplicity is often the best approach. Get help if necessary. Never let your guests think you're huffing and puffing: panic is contagious.

BE PRACTICAL. Emily Post advised a "pragmatic approach"—everything she did was geared to common-sense practicality. Stick with what you know. Don't experiment on your guests; in other words, don't serve something you haven't made before or plot an elaborate evening you're ill-equipped to handle.

BE REALISTIC. Work within your budget. Cut back on the size of your guest list if necessary. You don't have to buy luxury foods or wines or prepare a fancy, complicated dish to have a successful party.

BE PREPARED. Plan your menu well in advance and plot out the time it will take to prepare each dish.

Prepare what you can in the days before the party; many items freeze well. If, for example, you are planning to serve a crabmeat dip in pastry puffs, you can make the puffs weeks before and freeze them.

INVITE A CONGENIAL MIX OF GUESTS. Guests who enjoy being together—whether old friends or new—will add the extra zip that makes any occasion a memorable one.

CHAPTER 1

THE GOOD HOST

To entertain successfully, always plan ahead. With thorough preparation, your fine occasion will be a labor of love not only for your guests but also for you. There is nothing more uncomfortable than for guests to feel that their host and hostess are running themselves ragged entertaining them. If you want your guests to be relaxed, you should relax, too. And you will be relaxed if you've done the bulk of the work ahead of time.

THE GOOD HOST'S PARTY GUIDE

There is nothing mysterious about hosting well. It involves little more than common courtesy, a nurturing ambiance, and a sincere interest in making guests feel comfortable and welcome.

BE RELIABLE. Be ready at the hour of the invitation. Don't count on late arrivals and rush to the door with your hair half-dried or a dust rag in your hands when guests arrive at the hour at which you've invited them.

BE AVAILABLE. Be there to greet guests as they arrive, even if you have to excuse yourself from a conversation with another guest. It is not necessary for both the host and hostess to greet guests at the door.

BE PREPARED. Have the table set in advance, and plan meals that do not require you to spend the entire cocktail hour in the kitchen.

BE PRECISE. Be clear in your invitation as to the formality of the occasion. Don't write "casual" and open the door wearing satin and diamonds.

BE A CATALYST. Make a point of circulating among your guests and introducing strangers to one another, staying with them long enough to get a conversation launched.

BE AWARE. Keep an eye on guests' drinks, offering refills so that they don't have to ask.

BE A LEADER. Remember that guests look to you to raise your fork first during dinner; do so promptly so that they may begin eating. Or be sure to say, after the first three or so guests are served, "Please begin eating," so that the food doesn't cool while they wait for you to be served or to serve yourself.

BE MINDFUL. Pay attention to details, such as a well-stocked bathroom. A hostess should have guest towels hanging in plain view. Because people often consider linen hand towels to be decorative only, have terry hand towels available. Or place a small stack of nice paper towels beside the sink, to throw away into a wastebasket afterward. Have plenty of extra toilet paper on hand, and a fresh bar of soap in the soap dish.

CHAPTER 2

THE GOOD GUEST

A good guest is enthusiastic, congenial, and considerate, treating other guests and the host and hostess, as well as their property, with thoughtfulness and respect. The most well-mannered guest at any occasion follows the rules of the Good Guest's Party Guide, below.

THE GOOD GUEST'S PARTY GUIDE

KNOW WHEN TO ARRIVE. If the invitation is a casual "come at 6:30 or 7:00," split the difference and ring the bell at 6:45, but never later than 7:00. On the other hand, if you have ever arrived at 6:15 to find your hostess just out of the shower, you know it is safe to say that one should never arrive early at this hostess's house. When a specific time is given, arrive at the time stated, or shortly thereafter. Be especially attentive to time if yours is a dinner-party invitation. The smart host never lets a late guest disrupt the dinner-party schedule. Fifteen minutes is the established length of time to delay dinner—if a guest is later than that, he should not be surprised to find other guests seated and the dinner underway.

TAKE SPECIAL CARE NOT TO DAMAGE YOUR HOST'S PROPERTY. If it is muddy or wet outside, wipe your feet on the doormat. Don't put your feet up on the couch or the coffee table. Don't fiddle around with knickknacks or table ornaments. Put your drink glass on a coaster or ask for one if none is in sight.

DO NOT SNOOP. It is rude to tour through someone's house uninvited. Ask your host if he will show you the house.

COMPLY WITH THE HOSTS' PLANS. Don't ignore your hostess when she announces that dinner is served. On the other hand, don't jump up and fly out as if you have been kept waiting to the point of starvation. Watch your hostess, and if she seems to be edging toward the door, take one more sip of your cocktail and rise.

DO NOT SMOKE IN ANYONE'S HOME UNLESS THEY DO SO THEMSELVES. Today, with unanswered questions about the dangers of secondhand smoke, even those who didn't mind previously may mind now. If you must have a cigarette, ask your host or hostess if you can step outside for a few minutes. Never light a pipe or cigar indoors without asking first. Never smoke around infants or small children. When at a party in a club where smoking is allowed, it is still courteous to ask those with you if they mind if you smoke. Lastly, it is bad form to walk around or dance with a cigarette in your hand or hanging from your mouth.

CONFESS TO A PROBLEM YOU'VE CREATED. If you burn the surface of a table or a rug, break an ornament, or snap the back legs of the chair, don't try to hide the damage. Apologize at once and arrange to replace the item if possible or to pay for repairs if not. If it is a substantial amount, see if your personal insurance policy will cover it.

DON'T USE THE TELEPHONE WITHOUT PERMISSION. Then only use it if you charge the calls to your credit card or home number. If you have a cell phone, don't use it without first asking if your host minds if you make a call. Simply excuse yourself to make your calls in the privacy of the guest room. Don't forward personal calls to your host's house without asking permission to do so and then only if you are an on-call professional or are anticipating an emergency call.

NEVER VISIT FRIENDS WHEN YOU HAVE A COLD OR OTHER INFECTIOUS ILLNESS. No matter how bored you are staying home alone with a cold or cough, home is indeed where you ought to stay. If you're home sick and want companionship, pick up the telephone or, if you own a computer, catch up on some e-mail.

PRACTICE BATHROOM ETIQUETTE. If you use a hand towel, make sure to put it back on the rack, unfolded, so that it is obvious that it has been used. When you wash your hands, wipe off the basin. Before you leave, put the toilet seat and the lid down.

THE GLOBAL GUEST

You may be the most polished executive in your company and a confident globetrotter, but without knowing the nuances in cultural practices and customs in a foreign country it is easy to appear ignorant when you are a guest there. Differences in mores, cultural practices, decision-making, and the way people converse can trip up even the most seasoned traveler. It is the wise guest who takes the time not only to understand these differences but to practice them as well. As the saying goes, when in Rome, do as the Romans do.

Here are some basic courtesies to keep in mind when you are a guest in a foreign land.

- Don't criticize the way things are done in the host country or make comparisons to your own country.
- Be prompt and punctual.
- Follow the standards of dress and grooming in the host country. Conservative is always better. In many countries, women should not wear pants, skirts above the knee, or tops that expose the arms or have a deep neckline.
- Be prepared to shake hands frequently, especially in Europe. In many countries women do not shake hands regularly; in those situations, wait for the woman to extend her arm to you for a handshake, whatever your gender.

TAKING LEAVE

It was once a fixed rule that the guest of honor should be the first to leave the party. This rule is more or less obsolete, however, unless the guest of honor is the president of the United States or other dignitary, in which case no one leaves before he or she does. In all other circumstances, guests may depart before the guest of honor does.

When should a guest go home? Dinner guests should *stay at least one hour after dinner*, since it is hardly a compliment to the hostess when her guests do little more than eat and run. At a small party, a couple should not leave long before anyone else seems ready to go, because their departure is very apt to break up the party.

Today it is not considered ill-mannered for any couple or individual to rise if the hour is growing late. If you are a guest and it is late, and you are ready to leave, simply stand up, say good-bye to the people with whom you were talking, say good-bye to the guest of honor, and look for your hostess. Chat for a brief moment with her and the host, and then offer your thanks and good-byes, and leave.

- Show respect for older persons. Stand when they enter the room, wait for them to speak first, and wait for them to initiate a handshake.
- Do not immediately call someone by his or

her first name. It's largely an American custom,
so only do so when you're invited.
- Respect your host's dietary customs; don't
  request something that may be offensive or
  contrary to his practices.

CUSTOMS AROUND THE WORLD

The following is a sampling of customs that are
specific to certain countries. While the burgeoning
global culture is infiltrating all corners of the globe,
many traditions survive and thrive in social interaction.

Arab and Islamic Countries

Never point or beckon with your fingers; these gestures are reserved for summoning animals. Arabs tend
to stand very close to the person to whom they are
speaking. Do not distance yourself. If a handshake is
accompanied by a kiss on both cheeks in social situations, return the gesture. Alcohol is forbidden and is
rarely consumed in public, although it may be served
at a private function. In many Arab countries, women
do not dine with men, even at a business dinner, so
this should be expected.

China

Bow your head slightly when introduced, as a sign of
respect. Speak quietly, for loud voices are considered
rude. Follow your host's lead at a meal, neither eating

nor drinking until he does. When a toast is given, it is the practice to empty one's glass each time. If you are not used to drinking, exercise caution when toasting with an alcoholic beverage, perhaps requesting a soft drink or water instead.

France

Address people formally. If you take a French host out to dinner or lunch, suggest that he select the wine, a point of pride with most French, and be sure to praise it.

Germany

Handshakes are formal and are often accompanied by a barely perceptible bow, but unless one knows the host well, other touching, such as hugging or cheek kissing, is not encouraged.

Great Britain

Address people formally, by title, and keep physical contact at a minimum. Handshaking is expected, but not embraces or other touching. Eat with delicacy—even small finger sandwiches are to be eaten in little bites, never popped in their entirety into the mouth.

Israel

Dress in Israel is more informal than in many countries, with suit jackets left off and shirt sleeves acceptable. Understand and observe dietary restrictions, which are generally kosher; and understand religious observances, which take precedence over everything else. It is correct to say *shalom* for both hello and good-bye.

Italy

When dining, plan on several courses, and know that salad is served after the main course, not before. Coffee is generally served black, so you might want to adjust your taste buds if you are used to adding milk or cream to yours.

Japan

Formality is of the utmost importance; chatting or overt friendliness is not appropriate. Punctuality is also important. Handshaking is not as widely practiced as in other countries, and you should bow only if someone bows to you. Remove your shoes upon entering a Japanese home and most restaurants, placing them facing outward. If house slippers are provided, put them on. When you use the bathroom, remove the house slippers you are wearing outside the bathroom door and put on the pair outside the door that is provided to be worn into the bathroom.

Latin America

Handshakes and embraces are frequent, and people stand closer together than most North Americans are used to when speaking; don't back away—it's impolite. When invited to social functions, be prepared to dine quite late.

Russia
Punctuality counts in Russia, so it is a good idea to know where you are going and how long it will take you to get there.

Scandinavian Countries
Punctuality is important, as is privacy, and both should be respected. When offered a drink, accept it, but do not touch it until your host proposes a toast.

Spain
Time and punctuality are not always adhered to, so it is a good idea to be prepared to wait and not to criticize when you are kept waiting.

HOSTING A FOREIGN VISITOR

When a foreign visitor who speaks little English is your guest in America, don't put him on the spot by choosing entertainments that are dependent on good language skills. Choose instead universal enjoyments such as music concerts or dance performances. Even better: Bring along a friend who is proficient in your guest's language.

CHAPTER 3

INVITATIONS

Invitations can be anything from a spontaneous same-day phone call to a formal wedding invitation sent four to six weeks in advance. The first invitation is made in person or by telephone, while the second is often elegantly printed and mailed. Both have guidelines, and both require immediate replies.

Whether you're mailing out printed invitations or phoning guests, timing is key. The following are general guidelines for timing your invitations to avoid sending them out too late or too early.

INVITATIONS BY TELEPHONE

When inviting close friends to an informal dinner, barbecue, or small gathering for cocktails or dessert and coffee, a telephone invitation is perfectly acceptable. Whenever issuing a telephone invitation, start right out with the facts: "Hi, Greg, we're having a few people in Saturday night for dinner. Can you join us?" Greg is then free to accept or decline.

In responding to a telephone invitation, it is rude to say, "I'll let you know," unless it is immediately followed by an explanation such as "I'll have to ask John if he has made any commitments for that weekend." You should get back to the caller as soon as possible—no longer than one day—with your response.

WRITTEN INVITATIONS

When the event is of a more formal nature or is planned to honor a special guest or to celebrate a particular event, the invitation is preferably sent by mail. Like any other form of correspondence, the form and content of a written invitation is a reflection of the sender, so take care to select invitations that convey the proper formality or mood of the event.

When invitations are sent out, *every* guest should receive one. This is not the place to save expenses by verbally inviting good friends and neighbors when invitations have been mailed to everyone else. Should the good friends and neighbors find out that others received a more formal invitation, they will feel as though they were last-minute, fill-in invitees, not on your original list of guests. Even best friends should reply in the same manner as everyone else when they receive an invitation.

ELECTRONIC INVITATIONS

The use of e-mail to convey messages has become as commonplace as calling on the telephone. In fact, that is exactly the way e-mail should be used when issuing invitations: as a replacement for the kind of casual invitation you would make by phone. You should not send invitations by e-mail for a fancy formal party or wedding. E-mail invitations should be sent for casual, informal get-togethers only.

THE RANGE OF INVITATIONS

INFORMAL DINNERS OR PARTIES. Preprinted commercial invitations available at stationery and card stores are perfectly acceptable and practical. Extremely casual invitations can be written on notepaper or an informal notecard, or extended by telephone or e-mail.

FORMAL DINNERS. Invitations may be engraved or written by hand in the third-person style. Formal invitations are often engraved on white or cream cards— either plain or bordered by plate-mark (a raised border in the paper). Hosts who want their guests to dress formally often indicate this on their invitations. The phrase *black tie* or *white tie* should appear in the lower right-hand corner of the invitations.

INVITATIONS TO LUNCH. Although invitations to lunch are often telephoned, an engraved card is occasionally used for an elaborate luncheon party, especially for one given in honor of someone. However, a formal invitation to lunch is more often in the form of a personal note or a store-bought invitation card. It is usually mailed at least two weeks in advance. Note: The word *luncheon* is used less often these days, having been largely replaced by the more informal *lunch*.

REPLIES AND REGRETS

RSVPS

The term *RSVP* is from the French phrase *répondez s'il vous plaît*, 'please respond' and is often included on invitations. If the return address on the envelope is not the same as the one to which the replies are to be sent, the address for replies must be written under RSVP in the left-hand corner of the invitation.

Anyone receiving an invitation with an RSVP included is *obliged* to reply as promptly as possible. How do you reply? Simply match the style of the invitation. On most occasions—for acceptances and when there is nothing special to say—the reply-in-kind rule holds. A formal, third-person invitation requires a reply in the third person. If you are a close friend who wishes to explain your refusal or to express your delight in the invitation, however, you may always write a personal note. When the RSVP is followed by a telephone number, do your best to promptly telephone your answer. If you can't get through to the host after several attempts, don't give up. Send a brief note or even a postcard saying, "We'll be there" or "So sorry, but we can't make it." Always address your reply to the person who issued the invitation.

If the invitation says "Regrets only," don't send or call unless you are declining to attend. Only call or write regarding an acceptance if you have something to discuss with the hostess. If there is no RSVP requested at all, you are not obligated to reply, but it is never wrong to do so. Any host or hostess will appreciate your effort.

ASKING FOR AN INVITATION

You should never ask for an invitation for yourself. Nor should you ask to bring an extra person to a meal or a party. When regretting an invitation, you can always explain that you are expecting a weekend guest, leaving it up to the host-to-be to invite your guest or not. The host has every right to refuse to do so. But if he is having a big buffet or a large cocktail party he may not mind—and may even welcome— you bringing a houseguest.

CHANGING YOUR ANSWER

FROM "YES" TO "NO." If a *real* emergency arises, and you find you cannot attend a function for which you have already accepted, let the hostess know immediately. If the occasion is a seated dinner or a bridge party, you'll need to do so at once, since the hostess will have to find a replacement right away. If the event is a large catered party, it is also important to let your hostess know of your change of plans immediately, because caterers generally charge for the number of guests expected and not for how many actually arrive. In the case of an open house or a big cocktail party, your cancellation is not so much a practical concern as it is one of common courtesy.

In most cases a telephone call is best; it's quick and gives you a chance to explain your problem and express your regrets in person. If you prefer, however, and if there is ample time, you may write a short note giving your reason and your apologies. If the affair is a formal one or a sit-down dinner, it is then perfectly fine for the hostess to ask a close friend to fill in. It should be a friend that would be flattered, not insulted, that the hostess feels comfortable asking for last-minute help.

FROM "NO" TO "YES." If you refuse an invitation for perfectly legitimate reasons and then find that circumstances have changed and you can attend after all, you may sometimes rescind your regrets. It all depends on the nature of the occasion. If the affair is a party of limited number, such as for a seated dinner, your spot has likely been filled. It would only embarrass the host if you ask to be reinstated. If, however, the party is a large reception, a cocktail buffet, a picnic, or any affair at which the addition of another guest or two will not likely cause any complications, you may call the host, explain your situation, and ask if you may change your regret to an acceptance.

PARTY WEAR

Dress-code suggestions do get confusing. Some hosts' and hostesses' descriptions are vague, and regions of the country have variations in customs. The rule of thumb in party wear: It is better to dress down (slightly) than up. Better yet, do some checking. Ask your hosts, or another guest, to clarify the type of clothing and degree of formality for the upcoming occasion.

WHAT TO WEAR?

People are often confused as to exactly what is meant when an invitation specifies a certain type of dress, from "dressy casual" and "business casual" to "white tie," "black tie," "formal," "semiformal," and "informal."

"INFORMAL" OR "COME CASUAL" means just that: something informal and comfortable but neat, pressed, and clean. Your attire should fit the custom of the area and occasion; for a poolside party, clean, neat jeans and a T-shirt, plus your bathing suit, would usually be fine.

THE TERMS "DRESSY CASUAL" AND "BUSINESS CASUAL"—while confusing—are becoming more prevalent. "Dressy casual" may seem a bit of a contradiction in terms; however, in these relaxed times, it may keep people from showing up in a T-shirt and torn cutoffs. For a "dressy casual" affair, wear something nicer than ordinary everyday casual clothes, but not as fancy as cocktail wear. "Business casual" usually means wearing something a little more casual than customary office attire, such as khakis, sports shirts, and blazers or sweaters.

"SEMIFORMAL" generally means that women wear dresses or dressy pants ensembles. Men wear either suits and ties or sports shirts, a sports jacket, a tie, and slacks. If in doubt, it is perfectly acceptable for you to check with your hostess.

"BLACK TIE" OR "FORMAL" means men should wear tuxedos with a soft shirt and bow tie. Jackets may be white in the summer and black the rest of the year, and are available in patterns and many other colors. Women either wear long dresses, or a short, cocktail-length dress, depending upon what is currently customary in their area or culture and for the occasion.

"WHITE TIE" is the most formal evening wear—for men, white tie, wing collar, and tailcoat. This is almost never required today, except for official and diplomatic occasions and the rare private ball. For a woman, "white tie" indicates that a long gown should be worn.

INVITATION ENCLOSURES

You may need to include in your invitations other pieces of information for the guest. Enclosures are

WHEN DO THE INVITATIONS GO OUT?

General Guidelines:

Formal dinner
3 to 6 weeks

Informal dinner
From a few days away
to 3 weeks

Cocktail party
2 to 4 weeks

Anniversary party
3 to 6 weeks

Thanksgiving dinner
2 weeks to 2 months

Christmas party
1 month

Bar mitzvah
At least 1 month

Graduation party
3 weeks

Bon voyage party
Last minute to 3 weeks

Housewarming party
From a few days
to 3 weeks

Luncheon or tea
From a few days to
2 weeks

placed in front of the invitation, which is inserted with the writing facing the flap side of the envelope, so that the recipient sees the writing on the invitation and any enclosures as the invitation is removed.

MAPS. If your home, your club, or the location of the party is unfamiliar to some guests or difficult to find, it is enormously helpful and courteous to draw a map of the best route to take. Or you can write out the directions. Have the map or instructions reproduced, and enclose them with your invitations.

SCHEDULE OF EVENTS. This may be used when the weekend of a big wedding or event has multiple gatherings at different venues. Directions to the events are especially valuable to out-of-town guests.

TICKETS. When the invitation is to an event where tickets are required, such as a commencement, these tickets may be enclosed with the invitation if you know the recipient will be coming and the invitation is a formality.

RAFFLE TICKETS. Charity and fund-raising organizations often enclose raffle tickets with their invitations, hoping that even if the recipient cannot attend the event, he will purchase a raffle ticket and support the organization in that way.

RESPONSE CARDS. If you have chosen to send your guests response cards for their use in replying, the card and your self-addressed stamped envelope are enclosed in front of the invitation.

CHAPTER 4

SETTING THE TABLE

Most of us have little need these days for ten-course place settings. The American manner of entertaining is moving toward a more casual approach. Whether you call your dinner party "informal," "semiformal," or "casual," you have much more latitude in planning your table setting than you do for a formal dinner. Still, there are a few overall factors that should be given attention within the framework of your available space, your budget, the style of your home, your party's theme, and the tastes of your guests. Outside of those limitations, you should give your imagination and creativity free rein in setting a fine table.

INFORMAL PLACE SETTINGS

The main difference between the formal and informal place setting is that the latter requires less of everything. Fewer courses are served, so fewer pieces of silver and plates are set out.

The typical place setting for an informal three-course dinner would include the following. Notice that the silver to be used last is placed next to the plate.

TWO FORKS, one for salad at the far left and one for dinner to the left of the plate. (Note: It is also correct to place the salad fork to the right of the dinner fork if the salad is to be served after the entrée.)

DINNER PLATE, which should not be set on the table when guests sit down.

SALAD PLATE to the left of the forks.

ONE DINNER KNIFE next to the plate on the right. For steak, chops, chicken, or game, you may use a steak knife instead, and use a regular dinner knife in addition only if necessary.

TWO SPOONS—dessert spoon to the right of the knife and soup spoon at the far right.

ONE BUTTER PLATE WITH BUTTER KNIFE, if you have them.

ONE WATER GOBLET or tall tumbler.

ONE WINEGLASS if you plan to serve wine.

NAPKIN in the center of the place setting, or to the left of the forks.

TIPS FOR INFORMAL PLACE SETTINGS

Plan your place setting around your menu. If you serve bread and butter, try to include a butter plate in the place setting. Serve separate salad plates if your menu includes any dishes with gravy. Salad may be put on the same plate with broiled steak, chops, or chicken, but can be an unappetizing mess when combined with chicken gravy or lamb stew.

Generally, only one or two wines are served, so a water goblet and one or two wineglasses are all that are necessary. In the event that wine is not served, iced-tea glasses are often put out.

If you plan to serve coffee with the meal, the cup and saucer go to the right of the setting, with the coffee spoon placed on the right side of the saucer.

Service plates are not used at an informal dinner, except under soup bowls and under the stemmed glass used for shrimp cocktail and fruit cocktail.

The dessert spoon and fork (or, if you prefer, just a spoon) need not be beside the dinner plate. They can be brought in, as at a formal dinner, with the dessert plate, or they can be placed, American style, above the center of the place setting, horizontally, with the bowl of the spoon facing left and the tines of the fork facing right.

THE FORMAL TABLE SETTING

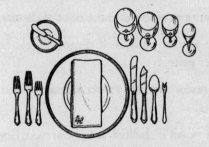

The one rule for a formal table is that everything should be geometrically spaced: the centerpiece in the actual center, the place settings at equal distances, and utensils balanced. Beyond this one rule you can vary your arrangement and decorations to a wide degree. A formal place setting generally consists of the following.

SERVICE PLATE positioned so the pattern "picture" faces the diner.

BUTTER PLATE placed above the forks at the left of the place setting.

WINEGLASSES positioned according to size.

SALAD FORK placed directly to the left of the plate.

MEAT FORK positioned to the left of the salad fork.

FISH FORK positioned to the left of the meat fork; since it is used first, it is to the outside left.

SALAD KNIFE, if one is provided, just to the right of the plate.

MEAT KNIFE placed to the left of the fish knife.

FISH KNIFE positioned to the right of the meat knife.

BUTTER KNIFE positioned diagonally at the top of the butter plate.

SOUP SPOON AND/OR FRUIT SPOON placed outside the knives.

OYSTER FORK if shellfish is to be served, beyond the spoons; this is the only fork ever placed on the right.

TIPS FOR FORMAL PLACE SETTINGS

Knife blades are placed with the cutting edge toward the plate.

No more than three of any implement is placed at the same time at each place setting (with the exception of the use of an oyster fork, which makes four forks). Therefore, if more than three courses are served before dessert, the fork for the fourth course is brought in with the course; or the salad fork and knife may be omitted in the beginning and brought in when salad is served.

Dessert spoons and forks are brought in on the dessert plate just before dessert is served.

A truly formal dinner generally has a tablecloth of white damask, under which you can place a felt pad or a folded white blanket to protect the table. The tablecloth for a seated dinner should hang down approximately 18 inches. It should not extend to the floor, as it would on a buffet table.

Formal dinner napkins should match the table-cloth. They are folded three times in each direction to make a smaller square. The two sides are then folded under, making a loosely rolled rectangle. The napkin is not flattened down completely. If there is a monogram, it shows at the lower left corner of the rectangle, or if the initials are at the center of one side of the napkins, they appear in the center third of the roll. Napkins are placed in the center of the service plate with the monogram facing the diner. They are put at the side when a first course is put on the table before seating the guests. If placed to the side of the plate, the napkins are not put under the forks, but rather to the left of them.

Each place is set with the number of glasses that will be used during the meal, with the exception of the dessert wineglass, which is put on the table after the dessert is served. Water goblets are placed closest to the center of each setting, with the wineglasses to the right in the order they will be used.

At most formal dinners two or three glasses in addition to the goblet are usual—one for sherry, one for a red wine, and one for a light white wine. Arrange wine-glasses according to size, so that little ones are not hidden behind large ones. The goblet for water is placed directly above the knives at the right of the plate; next to it, at a slight distance to the right, the champagne glass. In front and between these two, the claret or red wine-glass, or the white wineglass; then, either in front of this or somewhat to the right again, the sherry glass.

China may be mixed, but *all* the plates for each course should match.

Put pepper grinders and salt cellars at every place or between every two places. A set of salt-and-pepper shakers, if used instead, should be easily available to every diner; place sets two to three places apart. For a dinner of 12 there should be six (not less than four) salt-and-pepper shakers.

SEATING ARRANGEMENTS

Almost all seating problems can be worked out by employing common sense and consideration for your guests. The standard remains: Do what makes your guests most comfortable. Below are some general rules on proper seating arrangements for hosts and guests at a dinner party.

Seat honored guests at the host and hostess's right. If the party has a female guest of honor, the host seats her on his right.

When there is an uneven number of men and women, space them as evenly as possible. The hostess may keep her place at the end of the table unless doing so puts too many women in a row. At a formal dinner party, the woman next in importance sits at the host's left, and her husband, or the man of next importance, sits on the hostess's left.

When a single woman entertains at a large dinner, she seats the female guest of honor, if there is one, at one end of the table and herself at the other end. If a man is acting as host, he is seated to the woman of honor's left. The man of honor is seated to the hostess's right, and other guests are seated alternating men and women around the table.

When there is more than one table, the host should sit at one table and the hostess at another. If there are more than two tables, have a good friend act as a surrogate host, seeing that wine is served and plates refilled.

If someone is hard of hearing, consider how best to accommodate him, whether seating him with his best ear toward the conversation or beside people who speak clearly and forcefully.

Lefties, too, must be given elbow room; it is thoughtful to seat a left-handed diner at a corner where his left arm will not bump into the person beside him.

Avoid seating people next to each other who are deeply involved in, or rabidly opinionated about, opposite sides of a controversial issue. While a friendly difference of opinion or even a mild argument is often stimulating, a bitter controversy is embarrassing and destructive to good conversation. Remember the standard: Do what makes your guests most comfortable.

DECOR: SETTING THE MOOD

The American preference for casual entertaining does not mean your decor should look thrown together. In informal entertaining, "decorating" simply means having fewer restrictions and more options in giving your table a unique appeal. Take time to come up with a decor that meshes eye-pleasing colors, textures, and materials. You can decorate with:

LINENS. Match tablecloth, placemats, and napkins in a universal theme—whether of color, pattern, or shape.

CHINA AND GLASSWARE. Mix and match different sets of china and glassware, but make sure the disparate elements create a pleasing whole.

THE CENTERPIECE. If yours is for a formal table, keep in mind the following guidelines:

Keep the centerpiece from overwhelming the table or being in the way of serving and dining.

Don't let your centerpiece block the views of people sitting across from one another.

CANDLES. The ambiance of a party can be greatly enhanced by soft, romantic lighting. Tip: It's a good idea to avoid overly aromatic candles at dinner parties—they can affect the taste of your food.

The number of candles you use depends on whether the room is otherwise lighted. If candles alone light a table, there should be one candle for every person. If the candles are used in addition to other lighting, two or four candles are adequate for a table of up to eight people.

Candles are used informally in candlesticks; for

formal dinners, candelabra are often used, although candlesticks are fine. Make sure your candles are high enough so that the flame is above the eye level of the diners. For formal dinners, the candles should be white and brand-new.

FLOWERS. There may be no centerpiece more glorious than one that includes flowers. For formal tables, flowers are often seen in two or four smaller vases or epergnes, in addition to a larger arrangement in the center.

TEN EASY CENTERPIECE IDEAS

1. Fill straw or wicker baskets with potted African violets.
2. Combine colorful seasonal fruit, such as bananas, apples, grapes, pears, and cherries, with shiny magnolia leaves in baskets.
3. Place white candles of varying heights atop a mirror. Or put votive candles in small glass containers on top of the mirror.
4. Put a long, clear glass candleholder into a clear glass vase. Fill the vase with marbles and place a candle into the candleholder. The light reflected through the marbles is truly magical.
5. At Christmas, fill clear glass bowls with Christmas ornaments and ribbon.
6. Place colorful candles atop Italian or Mexican tiles.

7. Place dried-flower or silk flower arrangements on a polished wood tabletop.
8. For a Valentine's Day table, float red or white votive candles in a large glass bowl and add red rose petals to float in the water.
9. Place a delicate medium-sized vase filled with fresh-cut flowers in the center of the table, and put a small two- to three-inch vase with one or two delicate fresh flowers at each diner's place setting.
10. At Thanksgiving, fill a large wooden bowl with gourds, squashes, and Indian corn.

PART II

PARTIES AND EVENTS

The major forms of entertaining are generally some variation of Cocktail Party, Dinner Party, and Buffet. When choosing among "The Big Three," consider which format best matches the purpose of your party.

CHAPTER 5

THE COCKTAIL PARTY

In many circles, cocktails are back in fashion. Favored drinks of the forties to the early sixties—concoctions such as the martini, the Old-fashioned, and the Manhattan—are seeing a revival. Along with the new interest in cocktails is the resurgence of cocktail parties. In many parts of the country, cocktail parties have become the most common form of entertaining and the answer to a busy person's quandary. They provide a relatively simple solution to the rule that all invitations must be repaid. Keep in mind these tips when planning a cocktail party:

INVITATIONS

If the number of guests is small, the invitation is almost always by telephone. For a larger party, invitations are usually written on a printed fill-in card or on an attractive store-bought card.

Unless you are having a cocktail buffet, the time is usually stated on the invitation: "Cocktails *from* 5:00 P.M. to 7:00 P.M.," rather than "Cocktails *at* 5:00 P.M."

While "RSVP" is often omitted, thoughtful guests let their host and/or hostess know whether or not they are planning to attend the party.

COCKTAIL-PARTY FOOD

Think finger food: one-bite foods, mini-appetizers, and morsels that can be picked up with a toothpick are all perfect cocktail party foods.

Small plates and forks are generally not necessary. It makes it difficult for guests to hold a drink and plate and eat at the same time. Have plenty of paper napkins lying around.

Opt for a cocktail buffet. A cross between a cocktail party and a buffet dinner party, the cocktail buffet is the choice of many for entertaining all but the smallest and most informal groups. Because a cocktail buffet generally has plenty of food, guests won't need to make plans for dinner and can linger longer at the party. The main difference between a cocktail buffet and a buffet dinner is that only one real course is served at a cocktail buffet.

COCKTAIL-PARTY BEVERAGES

Generally, the host and hostess serve as bartender and server. As each guest arrives, ask what he would like to drink. Invite him to refill his glass if he wants another.

If you are planning a cocktail party for more than 18 or 20 people, it is wise to consider hiring a bartender for the evening. One bartender can serve between 20 and 30 people quite nicely. If the party is larger, you may want to hire two bartenders and locate each at separate bar areas—the crush around one can become unmanageable.

If you have two bars, you can designate one as strictly a cocktail bar and the other for wine, beer, and nonalcoholic drinks only.

If you hire a bartender, ask him to use a jigger for measuring quantities. A jigger measures out a precise 1.5 ounces of liquor, the standard serving for cocktails and highballs. (If you let your bartender measure by eye, you may find that your liquor supply is about to run out long before the cocktail hour is over.) Ask him as well to wrap a napkin around each glass to prevent drips and make holding a wet, icy glass more comfortable. Have plenty of coasters in sight to prevent water damage to tabletops.

THE WELL-STOCKED BAR

As a general rule, count on each guest's having at least three drinks. A one-quart bottle will provide 21 1 ½-ounce drinks or serve approximately seven people. Most liquor stores will let you return unopened bottles, so always buy a bit more than you need. Don't forget the nonalcoholic drinks, including tomato and fruit juices, a choice of sodas, and sparkling mineral waters. It's important to base your selections on what you know about your guests' preferences. Many people these days prefer wine to hard liquor, for example.

At a large party have plenty of extra glasses on hand. Guests continually put down their glasses and forget where they put them, or leave their empty ones behind when they go to the bar for another drink. Plastic glasses are perfectly fine—and perfectly practical—to use for a big party. And don't forget perhaps the most important ingredient: ice, and plenty of it!

The well-stocked bar should include:

Mixers and fixings. Lemons, limes, olives, tonic, seltzer or club soda, sweet and dry vermouth, bitters, orange juice, tomato juice, grapefruit juice.

Paper/plastic goods. Napkins, glasses, toothpicks, coasters.

Essential accouterments. Jigger, corkscrew, swizzle sticks, bottle opener, bar towel, ice bucket, cocktail spoon or stirrer, paring knife, cocktail picks.

For every ten guests have:

Three fifths each of vodka, scotch, and bourbon—
    or the liquors favored by your guests.
Five bottles of wine.
Five six-packs of beer.
Five six-packs of soda.

TEN EASY COCKTAIL PARTY
HORS D'OEUVRES

You don't have to spend hours in the kitchen in order to have delicious, enticing food at your cocktail party. All of the following hors d'oeuvres can be prepared ahead of time or at the last minute.

- Mozzarella balls marinated in basil and oliveoil.
- Mini ham biscuits with honey mustard.
- Sun-dried tomato and sour cream dip with cut-up raw vegetables.
- Deviled eggs with a dollop of salmon roe (inexpensive) or caviar (expensive).
- Smoked salmon and cream cheese on mini toast pieces or thin slices of pumpernickel.
- Spicy cheese sticks.
- A dip of artichokes, mayonnaise, and Parmesan cheese served with crackers.
- Homemade salsa and chips.
- Potato chips, pretzels, and trail mix.

CHAPTER 6

THE DINNER PARTY

Whether your dinner party is held in a restaurant, a club, or your own home, and whether there are a hundred guests or eight, the requisites for a successful occasion are the same. They include:

GUESTS who are congenial.

A MENU that is well planned and suited to your guests' tastes.

AN ATTRACTIVE TABLE with everything in perfect condition: linen pressed, silver polished, and glassware sparkling.

FOOD that is well prepared.

A GRACIOUS AND CORDIAL HOSTESS AND HOST, who are welcoming and at the same time enjoy their guests.

Most well-planned dinner parties go off without a hitch. Fiascoes, however, do happen to everyone sooner or later. No matter what occurs, it's all about making a gracious recovery—whether for your guests or for yourself—and keeping a sense of humor.

We've all experienced the ice-cold ovens and the collapsing soufflés. If dinner falls flat, just order a couple of pizzas and put your feet up; the whole evening will be next year's dinner-party anecdote.

TIPS FOR A SUCCESSFUL DINNER PARTY

The best hosts make it look so easy no matter what happens. Here is some gold-plated advice on preparing food for a smashing dinner party:

Plan ahead.

Serve something you've served before.

Have a fallback: If the dessert soufflé falls, have ice cream and fudge sauce in the kitchen as a backup.

Lists are essential. Make a list of all your grocery needs. Make a list of all your cooking needs: one for pots and pans and another for spices. Make a list of all your china and glassware needs. Make a list of all courses, and locate the serving dish and utensils in which you plan to serve each course.

Don't set the table at the last minute. Do so the night before or the morning of the party.

Using a variety of china patterns is a popular trend. Try to use dishes that share a similar color, pattern scheme, or linking design element. The secret is not in having everything of one design, but in creating, out of a variety of patterns, colors, and textures, a harmonious whole.

When you are entertaining a large group, you might want to use placecards to let each guest know where they are to sit at the dinner table and to mix and match people for best effect. Placecards are a good way to introduce people who don't know each other and may be as formal or informal as you like.

Even the most organized hostess needs help now and then. Hire temporary help or a neighborhood teen to come in during course changes and wash dishes.

When choosing your dinner-party menu, always strive to plan a well-balanced meal. Combine flavors intelligently. Don't serve heavy or spicy dishes back to back.

A second consideration is the appearance of the food you serve. Color is as important in devising your menu as it is in planning your decor.

Consider the season as well. Light foods, such as main-course salads and cold soups, are perfect warm-weather fare. Heavy foods, such as stews and roasts, warm the soul in winter. Make use of the season in another way by creating a menu using fresh seasonal foods.

Finally, think about the limitations of your kitchen. If your space is limited, prepare what you can ahead of time and plan your cooking times carefully so that no dish is delayed by a shortage of mixing, cooking, or carving space.

THE INFORMAL DINNER PARTY

BEVERAGES

When predinner drinks or cocktails are served, dinner should be planned for at least an hour later than the time noted on the invitation; twenty minutes later if drinks are not served, which allows late arrivals a moment of relaxation. Generally, your guests should have time for one or two cocktails. Many dinner parties with a cocktail hour also offer light snacks or hors d'oeuvres with the drinks.

After-dinner coffee may be served either at the dining table or in another room to which the diners have moved. Customarily, the hostess pours the coffee (and sometimes tea) right at the dining-room table or from a tray that has been carried to the living room or den.

Some hosts like to serve after-dinner drinks with coffee. If coffee is served at the table, bottles of after-dinner drinks may also be placed on the table, often on a tray holding a variety of glasses.

DINNER IS SERVED

When dinner is ready to be served, the candles are lit and water glasses are filled. You might want to start with a first course. If it is not a hot dish, try to have the first course already served at each diner's place. Then simply announce that dinner is served.

At a casual dinner party, guests may serve themselves or pass the food around the table for serving. Each dish is supplied with whatever silver is needed for serving it. Dishes are passed counterclockwise to the right and should be passed in the same direction, simply to keep the process orderly.

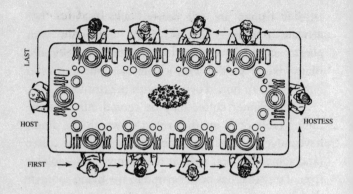

Order of Service

The female guest of honor seated on the host's right is always served each dish first. The hostess is never served first.

When food is served directly from the kitchen, service is counterclockwise from the female to the host's right, with the host served last. Plates are served from the guests' left side and removed, if possible, from the right. (An easy way to remember this is "RR"—remove right.)

Since any of these procedures can take considerable time—time in which the food can grow cold—it is important that the host or hostess insist that guests start eating after three or four people have been served.

When the table is cleared by the hostess alone or with a close friend assisting, dishes are removed two at a time. Don't stack or scrape the dishes at the table.

Salad plates as well as the plates used for the entrée are removed before dessert is served. Any salt-and-pepper shakers, unused flat silver, and dishes of nuts are taken off (on a serving tray, if you like).

THE FORMAL DINNER PARTY

Today, in these most informal times, almost any dinner where guests are seated at a dining-room table and served by someone other than themselves is considered a formal dinner. For most of us, a formal dinner does not require adherence to the kind of official protocol practiced in diplomatic circles; it simply provides a framework around which to develop your own brand of entertaining. By taking the suggestions that appeal to you, by eliminating the details that would be unnatural or difficult for you, and by combining the elements that are suitable to your home and your friends, you can use the information that follows just as it should be used—as a guide. It is far less important to have matching silver or fine goblets than it is to be a warm, relaxed, and gracious party-giver.

SERVING HELP

At a small formal dinner, one server can handle everything himself; or, if he has a server to help him, he passes the principal dishes and the server follows with the accompanying dishes.

At a very formal dinner served by a staff, one

server generally stands at the ready behind the hostess's chair, except when pouring wine.

FORMAL DINNER COURSES

Six courses are the maximum for even the most elaborate formal dinner. They are:

SOUP, FRESH FRUIT CUP, SLICED MELON, OR SHELLFISH (such as clams, oysters, or shrimp).

FISH COURSE, unless shellfish is served first.

THE ENTRÉE or main course (usually roast meat or fowl and vegetables).

THE SALAD, which is served between the entrée and the dessert. This is correct, in spite of the custom in almost all American restaurants of serving salad as a first course. Unless you know that a group of friends prefer it first, salad should be served toward the end of the meal or may be served with the entrée, on a separate salad plate.

DESSERT. There are two methods of serving dessert. One is to put the dessert fork and spoon on the dessert plate. If the dessert is served in a glass bowl, the bowl is placed on the plate before it is served. If finger bowls are used, they are brought on another plate after dessert has been served. Another formal way to serve dessert is to bring the finger bowl, as well as the fork and spoon, on a small doily on the dessert plate. The diner puts the finger bowl, on the doily, to the left above his plate and places the fork and spoon to the sides of the place setting. After dessert, the diner dips his fingers, one hand at a time, into the water and then dries his fingers on his napkin.

When fresh fruit is to be served, it is passed after the dessert, and decorative sweets, such as mints, are passed last.

COFFEE can be served with after-dinner drinks.

A WINE PRIMER

Wine with dinner is one of the great pleasures of communing with friends; used with taste and decorum, wine or champagne nicely complements and balances the flavors of a meal. Yet many novice hosts consider choosing a wine to be a daunting proposition. It doesn't have to be; simply ask your local wine merchant for advice. Here are some basic tips on buying, serving, and enjoying wine.

Taste before you buy. Most of the time, the wine that tastes best to you will also taste great to your guests.

The two most important considerations in choosing a wine are not the cost or where it came from, but that its flavors complement the food with which it is served and that it pleases the palates of the people drinking it. Although the tradition of serving a particular wine with a particular food is no longer de

rigueur, the fact remains that red wines nicely complement a bold sauce or a hearty roast pork, while white
and rosé wines neatly balance chicken and seafood
dishes. Of course, unless the meal is strictly formal,
there is no reason why the host may not choose any
wine he thinks his guests would prefer.

When buying wine, shop around. Prices can vary
greatly from one wine store to another. Look for spe-
cials in your local newspaper. Many stores offer a discount (generally ten percent) when you buy by the case
(twelve bottles per case). If you find you like a particular wine, you might want to consider buying it at a good
price, by the case. Another way to buy good wine at
reduced prices is to go to the source. Wineries are crop-
ping up in most regions of the country, and visiting one
on a tasting tour makes for a fine weekend excursion.

If you're serving wine at a dinner party, plan on
buying at least one bottle of wine per every two
guests. Of course, this is dependent on the number of
people you know will drink wine with dinner and an
estimate of how much they usually drink.

Once a bottle is opened, the wine should be
drunk within a day or so—oxidation causes wine to
rapidly deteriorate. To give wine a couple more days
of drinkability, you might pour it into a smaller bottle
or use one of several new gadgets that actually pump
the oxygen out of the bottle and reseal it. Otherwise,
you can use leftover wine in cooking.

If more than one wine is to be served during dinner, set a glass for each wine.

The general rule in serving several types of wine is: whites before reds, dry before sweet.

Don't "fill 'er up": When pouring wine, fill the wineglass only halfway, never to the top of the glass, to allow the wine to breathe.

Pick up your wineglass by the stem rather than the bowl. In the case of white wine and champagne this helps keep the wine cool. In the case of all wines, including red wines, holding it by the stem also lets you better appreciate the color.

White wine glass

Store wine bottles in a cool, dark place, preferably on their sides.

White wines should be served chilled—around 45°F—but never ice cold, which tends to overwhelm the taste. Serve white wine in tulip-shaped, stemmed glasses.

Red wines, for the most part, are served at a cool room temperature, preferably the same temperature it would be if kept in a wine cellar—approximately 60°F to 65°F. Serve red wines in round-bowled, stemmed glasses that are wider at the rim than white-wine glasses.

Red wine glass

Sparkling wines, which shine at celebrations of all sorts, come in

flute glass

coupe glass

many forms, from the sparkling white wine known as champagne to sparkling rosé wines and sparkling burgundies. Champagne, above all other beverages, is emblematic of a very special occasion. Champagne of nonvintage quality can be placed in the refrigerator for a day and then chilled further in a cooler filled with ice and a pinch or two of salt. Occasionally hold the bottle by the neck and turn it back and forth a few times. Take care not to leave the bottle in the salt and ice for a long time, or the champagne may be transformed to sherbet; check it regularly. When opening, be sure to wrap the bottle in a towel or napkin as protection in case the cork ejects too fasts and champagne spills over.

An excellent vintage champagne, on the other hand, ideally should be packed in ice without salt, which chills it just a little less.

Serve champagne in one of two types of champagne glasses, *coupe*-shaped or flute.

THE SERVICE PLATE AND HOW TO USE IT

At a formal dinner, from the time the table is set until it is cleared for dessert, a plate remains on the table at every place. The meal starts with a service plate (also referred to as a charger), a large plate usually twelve inches in diameter. The service plate at each place is a base for the first course, which is served on a separate plate that is put on top of the service plate. When the first course is cleared, the service plate remains until the hot plate with the entrée is served, at which time the two plates (the service plate and the entrée plate) are exchanged.

Service plate

NUMBER OF GUESTS

There is no set rule for the number of dinner guests you can comfortably serve yourself. It used to be that eight people was the maximum number you could serve on your own at a sit-down dinner. You can certainly cook for as many guests as you want, but to serve a seated dinner of more than eight efficiently and quickly, you may want to either change a sit-down dinner to a buffet or enlist a friend to help you serve. For more than sixteen, you may need two friends or temporary help. You'll need someone to help serve drinks, pass hors d'oeuvres, serve dinner, and clean up in the kitchen. Greater numbers generally require more help.

CHAPTER 7

THE BUFFET

Hosting a buffet is, in today's parlance, entertaining interactively. There are three great advantages to a buffet dinner that appeal to all of us. First, you can accommodate many more guests than your dining room table will seat. Second, because a buffet is truly a do-it-yourself party, lack of service is no handicap. And third, a buffet is blessed with the informality that many of us prefer today.

THE BUFFET TABLE

Buffet table

Set your buffet table as formally or informally as you wish. A table set with a white damask cloth, elegant silver candelabra, and a vase of white roses has all the hallmarks of a formal buffet. On an informal buffet, you can let your creativity run wild, combining colorful linens with flowers and greenery and beautifully arranged food.

If the party is large and the room is big enough, it is better to leave the table in the center of the room so that two lines of guests may serve themselves on both sides of the table at once. Divide each dish into two platters, and mirror them on either side of the table. First divide the main course into two parts, and place one platter or casserole at each end of the table. Plates are set in two stacks beside each platter, and napkins and silver neatly arranged next to each set of plates. Place twin dishes of vegetables, salads, bread and butter, and sauces and condiments on both sides of the table so that guests need only pass down one side. If the table is set against the wall, place your plates and main dish at the end that makes for the best flow of traffic.

THE BUFFET MENU

The foods you select for your buffet should be easy to eat with fork alone.

Avoid choosing dishes that are soupy, that wilt or collapse over time, or that need to be cut up or buttered.

Have a helper keep vigilant watch on the buffet

table to refill food platters and dishes. Have your refills ready to serve.

If you are a guest at a buffet, don't let your eyes overrule your stomach; help yourself to small portions, and if you're still hungry, you can get seconds later.

If you are serving hot food, an electric hot plate or tray is recommended. Make sure, however, that cords are not a trip hazard for guests.

Get around the hot-plate dilemma by offering food that can be eaten at room temperature or chilled. Try cold salmon with dill sauce, pasta or seafood salads, or cold roast beef topped with horseradish sauce.

BUFFET BEVERAGES

Place beverages and glasses on a separate sideboard or nearby table, if possible. If you are having a seated buffet, place water glasses on the tables and fill them before the guests sit down. Wineglasses should also be at the guests' places, but should never be filled in advance. The host (or a server) passes the wine when everyone is seated, or an opened bottle of wine can be placed on each table, to be poured by the person nearest to it.

If coffee is on the sideboard, guests may serve themselves at any time. Or the host or hostess can take a tray set with cups, a coffeepot, cream, and sugar into the living room to serve after dinner.

CHAPTER 8

LUNCHES, BRUNCHES, AND TEAS

LUNCHES

Lunches these days are often informal affairs hosted by more than one person. A lunch is the perfect way to entertain casually outdoors on a sun-filled porch, to celebrate a mother-to-be over light fare and desserts, to share a cherished tailgating ritual outside a sports stadium, or to combine a meal with a club or business meeting.

INVITATIONS

Invitations may be telephoned or, for more elaborate lunches given in honor of someone, sent on an engraved card. A formal invitation to lunch, however, is more often in the form of a personal note or on a fill-in invitation.

THE LUNCH MENU

Two or three courses are sufficient at any but the most formal lunch, and even then no more than four are served in a private home. A good way to plan your lunch menu is to select from the five possible courses listed on the following page:

FRUIT OR SOUP. If you're not serving fruit for dessert, melon, grapefruit, or a fruit cup is a popular first course. Serve the fruit cup in bowl-shaped glasses that fit into long-stemmed, larger ones with a space for crushed ice between, or in champagne glasses, after being kept cold in the refrigerator, or in individual bowls. Place the fruit cups on small serving plates.

A clear soup is a smart, light choice for starters. In the winter serve a hearty cream soup; in summer a chilled soup such as vichyssoise or gazpacho hits the spot. Some hosts like to serve a robust soup or stew as the main course. Serve soup with crackers or warm bread.

EGGS OR SHELLFISH. Egg and fish dishes often serve as the lunch's main course. If you offer an egg or shellfish dish, such as a hot seafood casserole, balance that with a light, simple meat dish, such as chicken salad on romaine lettuce, combining the meat and salad courses in one. On the other hand, if you first serve a light pasta, you could follow with meat and vegetables, as well as salad and dessert.

FOWL, MEAT (NOT A ROAST), OR FISH. This course is optional. If you do decide to serve a meat dish, balance it against the egg or shellfish dish you serve before, or combine it with the salad course. Don't discount sandwiches as too informal. Sandwiches can be as fancy as you make them. You can make a delicious lobster salad, for example, and serve it in a croissant. Place the roll on a bed of lettuce and surround it with colorful sliced vegetables. Voilà! You've made an exquisite lobster club sandwich plate.

SALAD. Salad is the mainstay of most lunch menus nowadays. Often, lunch consists merely of soup and a big plate of seafood or Cobb salad, garnished with crudités and breadsticks.

DESSERT. Go for a lighter touch than you would for a dinner party, particularly if a work meeting or a card game is scheduled after lunch. Ice cream and sorbet are always refreshing, especially with a splash of champagne and a dollop of raspberries or blueberries. Fresh fruit is an always-welcome palate pleaser; serve with mini lace cookies or chocolates.

LUNCH BEVERAGES

Have a pitcher of iced water or glasses of water already on the table if yours is a seated lunch.

Many hostesses serve coffee or tea during the meal instead of later. If you offer iced tea, decorate the glasses with sprigs of fresh mint and a lemon slice.

Unless the lunch is a business or club meeting, wine is often served. One wine is sufficient, and it should be a light one such as sauvignon blanc or a champagne. Wine spritzers (chilled white wine with soda) are also a nice light choice.

Cocktails may or may not be served before lunch. Lunch cocktails are generally lighter than those offered before dinner. A glass of white wine, a white-wine spritzer, a Bloody Mary, or a mimosa (champagne and orange juice) are typical prelunch drinks. As always, offer nonalcoholic drinks along with the cocktails.

THE INFORMAL LUNCH

At an informal lunch there are few restrictions regarding table settings. Napkins may certainly be made of paper. In fact, nicer paper napkins, particularly those that are dinner size and made to resemble damask or other fabric, are appropriate for all but formal table settings.

Candles are sometimes used as ornaments at the lunch table but should not be lit in the daytime.

If the occasion is a large lunch, guests are often seated at several card tables. Card tables may be covered with square tablecloths, plain or colored. A small flower arrangement makes a pretty centerpiece for each table.

At an informal lunch, you can serve the guests yourself, or let guests serve themselves family-style from large bowls or platters.

For a buffet lunch, the food is set out as for a buffet dinner, on the dining-room table or on any table with sufficient space. The fare, however, should be much simpler and lighter than for a dinner.

THE FORMAL LUNCH

The table setting for a formal lunch is identical to that of dinner. The plate service is also the same.

For a formal luncheon, the plain white tablecloth that is correct for dinner is used, although colored damask is also acceptable.

BRUNCHES

This popular form of casual entertaining is a combination of breakfast and lunch, but is generally held closer to the usual hour for lunch. Brunch is the perfect entertainment for spur-of-the-moment weekend gatherings: post-wedding celebrations among out-of-town guests, for example, or get-togethers with old friends who are in town for a special event or who are passing through the area on a business trip. Informality is the rule, in both dress and demeanor.

INVITATIONS

Invitations may be telephoned ahead of time, but this kind of party is so casual that the host may simply invite his friends as they are leaving another gathering.

THE BRUNCH MENU

The menu generally offers a choice of traditional breakfast and lunch dishes, alone or combined. Pair a mushroom omelet, for example, with ratatouille or a tomato salad. Or offer creamed chicken to serve over waffles.

BRUNCH BEVERAGES

Bloody Marys are a popular brunch drink, whether served with or without liquor. Also popular is the mimosa, an icy combination of champagne and chilled orange juice.

Don't forget to provide pitchers of fruit juices, pots of coffee or tea, and sodas.

TEA: THE REVIVAL OF A CLASSIC

Long considered the domain of the stodgy and fuddy-duddy, tea is back in style. Many hotels are offering afternoon teas, complete with tea sandwiches and desserts in comfortable living-room style settings. You can throw a cozy tea in your own home for just about any reason, whether to honor an out-of-town friend or new neighbor, to "warm" a new house, or to introduce a visiting relative.

INVITATIONS

Invitations to an informal tea are almost always telephoned. However, if the occasion is more formal, you may send a written invitation on either a fill-in card or personal notepaper.

TEATIME

Set a large tray at both ends of the table, one for tea and one for coffee. One tray is used to bring in all the equipment necessary for the proper serving of tea: a full pot of brewed tea, a pot with boiling water, tea bags if the tea is not made with loose tea, a milk pitcher, a sugar bowl, and thin slices of lemon. These days, herbal and decaffeinated teas are popular; include a selection for your guests.

For the coffee tray, provide a pitcher of milk or cream, a bowl of sugar, sugar substitutes, and lemon slices.

Place cups and saucers within easy reach of those who are pouring, usually at the left of the tray, because they are held in the left hand while the tea (or coffee) is poured with the right. If the person pouring is left-handed, she could, of course, reverse the order.

A tea bag should never be served in a cup of tea. Preferably, tea is steeped in a pot and then poured into cups and served. If you are given a cup with the tea bag floating inside, lift the bag from the cup with the spoon when the tea is the strength you like, hold it at the top of the cup while it drains, and place it on the saucer under the cup. Do not wind the string around the spoon and squeeze the tea bag dry.

TEATIME FOOD

You can serve your teatime food from a dining room table or a tea table set up in any room that has adequate space and easy access.

On either side of the table place stacks of little tea plates, with small napkins folded on each one.

Arrange behind these, or in any way that is attractive and uncluttered, the plates of food and necessary silver. Forks should be on the table if cake with soft icing is served.

Food for a tea party is quite different from that served at a cocktail party. For one thing, much of the food is sweet—cookies, cupcakes, scones, or slices of cake—and often bite-sized. In addition, most teas feature tea sandwiches, generally miniature cold sandwiches made on thin bread. In the winter you might welcome your tea guests with a tray of hot cheese puffs, pastries filled with mushrooms, or a warm artichoke dip. Sandwiches should be light and delicate, such as:

- Watercress and an herb mayonnaise rolled in thin bread
- A cucumber slice on a round of bread with a dollop of salmon roe
- Cream cheese on datenut bread
- Crabmeat salad on pumpernickel bread
- Smoked salmon and cream cheese on round toast

BREWING THE PERFECT CUP OF TEA

There is no magic involved in making a first-rate cup of tea. The most important part of the tea service? Boiling water, and plenty of it. To start, first fill a pot halfway with boiling water, let it stand a moment or two to heat the teapot, and then pour it out. Put in a rounded teaspoonful of tea leaves or one tea bag for each cup. Half this amount may be used if the tea is of superb quality. Then pour on enough *actually boiling* water to cover the tea leaves about half an inch. It should steep at least five minutes (or for those who like it very strong, ten minutes) before additional boiling water is poured on. When serving, pour half tea, half boiling water for those who like it weak. Increase the amount of tea for those who like it strong. The cup of good tea should be too strong without the addition of a little lively boiling water, which gives it freshness.

When tea has to stand a long time for many guests, the ideal way to keep it hot and tasting fresh is to make a strong infusion in a big kettle on the kitchen stove. Return the tea to the stove, letting the tea actually boil three to four minutes on the range; then pour it through a sieve or filter into your hot teapot. The tea will not become bitter, and it does not matter if it gets quite cold. The boiling water poured over no more than a tablespoon of such tea will make the drink hot enough.

CHAPTER 9

BUSINESS ENTERTAINING

These days, business and social life overlap in innumerable ways. For many people, work life is the wellspring from which social life develops. This often makes it hard to know when to separate the two. Because business and play have become increasingly interwoven, it is imperative that workers maintain a clear sense of where one ends and the other begins.

Socializing with business associates does offer a great opportunity to talk in a relaxed atmosphere, to cement relationships, and to get to know clients, employers, and employees better. Combining meals with business ensures that the flow of work continues uninterrupted during the workday.

ENTERTAINING OUTSIDE THE OFFICE

RESTAURANT BUSINESS MEALS

Sometimes there just aren't enough hours in the business day to get everything done without including breakfast, lunch, and dinner in the schedule. If your workday spills over into lunch or dinner, here are a few pointers to keep in mind.

When the invitation is yours, you can either ask your guest's choice of restaurants or give him a choice between two or three options. If he defers to your good judgment, select a restaurant that is close to your guest's office, or centrally located to both of you. Pick a restaurant with a low noise level and one where tables are spaced far enough apart to ensure privacy.

Make a reservation. Wasting time waiting in line just to be seated is just that: wasting time. Make every effort to arrive early, before your guest.

If you are the guest and you are the first to arrive, you may be shown to your table if there is a reservation—especially if the restaurant is full or filling up. Or you can wait in the foyer of the restaurant for your host to arrive.

Whether you are the host or the guest, you should stand to greet your party when they arrive.

Seat your guest in the preferred seat, generally the one that looks out at a view or into the restaurant.

Both the host and guest should order food that can be eaten easily while talking between bites. This is much more important than it sounds. Wrestling with a lobster (not to mention wearing a lobster bib!) may make you look more foolish than professional.

If you're having lunch, it's better not to drink alcohol. If you must, keep it to one drink. Business dining means business will be conducted, and you need your wits about you. If you're drinking at dinner, the same is true: Don't overdo it.

As host, you should indicate to your guest that he or she is welcome to order freely and without concern for cost by recommending something from the menu at the more expensive end of the price range. Or you can tell him what you will be having and even suggest he also choose an appetizer, clueing in your guest on how to order. If you are the guest, on the other hand, that doesn't mean you have the green light to run up the tab—always exercise restraint.

Time is precious: Be aware of your party's other obligations.

If you are the guest, do not attempt to snatch the check—the host pays. Only when two coworkers, at any level, agree to meet for lunch is the check split between them. Otherwise, it is assumed that the one inviting a guest is also the one who pays the check. The host also pays for checking the guest's coat.

BREAKFAST MEETINGS

Breakfast meetings are a great way for morning people who think best over a cup of coffee and break fast to start the day. Again, meetings should be held at a mutually convenient location and should be kept relatively short, since all concerned still have to get to the office. Breakfast meetings are particularly efficient when your professional agenda is short and your days are jam-packed with other meetings.

DINNER INVITATIONS

Business dinner invitations are less common than lunches since they obviously impinge on people's personal time. However, when executives are so busy that they cannot meet for lunch—or when there might be a special occasion to be handled over dinner—a business dinner may be arranged. A dinner invitation usually includes a group of people brought together for a common purpose.

Business dinner invitations should be extended well in advance. An executive's assistant may either telephone guests or write them a note saying, "Mr. Franklin would like to take Mr. Jones to dinner on the 27th," for example. Those without assistants make the invitations themselves in the same way. The invitation should be addressed to the businessperson only, at his office, so it is clear that the dinner is a business-related one and that spouses are not included. A reservation should be made at a convenient restaurant, at a quiet table or in a private room.

You as host must be there ahead of time to greet your guests, introduce them if they are not acquainted, and seat them at a table. Place the highest-ranking guest or the one due the greatest honor to your right; the second highest, to your left. Others may be seated at random. If everyone is on the same level, you might simply suggest that people sit anywhere they please.

You should order drinks when everyone arrives; if, however, someone is late, order anyway and let the latecomer catch up upon arrival. One or two predinner drinks is often the average.

ENTERTAINING IN THE OFFICE

CORPORATE DINING-ROOM ENTERTAINING

Employees of corporations and large companies often entertain in a corporate dining room on the office premises. The only differences between entertaining a guest at a restaurant and in the executive dining room are that menu choices are often limited—and there is no check at the end of the meal.

If the menu is preset, the host should ask his or her guests if they have any food preferences when extending the invitation. The host should be present to greet guests, take their coats, and direct them to restrooms.

When a group is being entertained, seating protocol is important. The most important guest sits to the host's right and the second most important to the host's left. If there is a second host, she sits opposite the host, with the third and fourth most-important guests to his right and left.

The host is responsible for conversation and for introducing the agenda at the appropriate time. He is also responsible for keeping conversation on the agenda once the business discussion begins.

It is up to the host to end the lunch by placing his napkin on the table and rising, once he or she is certain everyone is finished and the business discussion is concluded.

The host sees guests out, retrieving their coats and directing them to the elevator or stairs.

ENTERTAINING WITH SPOUSES AND PARTNERS

Most parties held at the office or during the workday do not include spouses or dates. Some occasions, however, do call for including spouses. These include:

- when out-of-town businesspeople and their spouses or partners visit in your area;
- when you return an invitation that included your spouse;
- when you want to get to know your client better;
- when the occasion to which you are extending the invitation is a couple's affair, such as a formal dinner or a dance;
- when you and a business associate find you have become friends and want to enjoy and share that friendship with your spouses;
- when you, as boss, wish to get to know your employees personally and have them know you as a person as well.

When you extend an invitation that includes spouses and partners, include your own; when you accept, accept for both of you. If you are the host but are unattached, invite a date; when you are a guest invited to a couple's event, you may ask if you can bring a friend. Couples who are unmarried but who live together should be treated exactly the same as married couples. Any party, whether at the office or at a private home, to which husbands and wives are invited should properly include any live-in partners. There are, of course, office parties to which spouses are not invited. Live-in partners should not be expected to attend those either.

If your partner has been excluded from an invitation because of the host's ignorance of your arrangement, just ask whether you may bring your partner along. Since good manners dictate that a live-in partner be invited to appropriate social occasions, the answer should be affirmative. If the reply is negative, however, you must decide whether you want to attend the affair alone or politely decline the invitation altogether.

ENTERTAINING AT HOME

When people invite business associates and clients to their homes, spouses are automatically included. Occasionally, a breakfast or lunch for business associates is held in someone's private home, but at those times the venue is generally chosen for convenience and privacy rather than a social occasion.

Again, if you are not married but are living with someone, your partner is treated the same as a spouse would be. If you are the host, a simple introduction of your partner is all that is needed as guests arrive.

The challenge to inviting a few business associates to your home is to do so without offending others at the office. Either invite those you've left off the list another time or keep the invitation private. Some employers make a ritual of inviting each member of their staff once during the year; some throw parties with small groups, others invite the entire staff at once. What you do depends on the accommodations your home can provide and the kind of entertaining that you and your spouse prefer.

GREETING GUESTS

If couples arrive and you haven't met your business associate's spouse, greet your coworker first with a handshake. Then quickly turn to his spouse (whose name you probably know at this point), and say something like, "Hello, Susan. I'm so happy to meet you." Your spouse should be close behind you as you greet them so that you may turn and say, "I'd like you to meet my wife [or husband]. Jennifer [or Michael], this is Eric Appleton and his wife, Susan."

At a small party, the host should then take his guests around the room, introducing them to people they do not know. In a large gathering, such as a cocktail party, business associates may assume this responsibility themselves, introducing their own spouses to their coworkers.

THE ROLE OF YOUR SPOUSE OR PARTNER

Your spouse, your home, and your entertaining style all reflect who you are and the choices you've made, and for better or worse, leave an indelible impression on those you work with every day. When you entertain at home, your spouse or partner is there to support you—to make your guests feel welcome, to help them enjoy being with you both, as well as to assist with refreshments. Since there will undoubtedly be a great deal of shop talk, it is your spouse's role to be interested—to listen, to ask questions, to indicate the involvement of both of you in the company. Even so, your husband or wife should feel free to discuss his or her profession and personal interests.

THE SINGLE HOST OR HOSTESS

If you are single and inviting business associates into your home, it's a smart idea to ask a friend to help you host the party. While it is by no means a requirement for a single person to have a stand-in host or hostess, it does make entertaining easier. Business entertaining at home is different from purely social entertaining in that a portion of the guests (the business associates) know each other well, while the rest of the crowd (generally spouses or dates) may not know each other at all. Having two hosts on duty eases the workload and allows the single host to give equal attention to spouses and dates.

When a single woman gives a business party, she may ask a close friend to act as host. One responsibility of the stand-in host may be to handle drinks—to either serve them, or see that guests are attended to by waiters or at a self-service bar. Another responsibility is to talk with guests, particularly with the spouses, who may feel out of place. Although the hostess will also be circulating to speak with guests, she may be busy making last-minute preparations and serving hors d'oeuvres or dinner.

The same logic applies when a single man hosts a business party. Similarly, it's a good idea to enlist a friend to help out. While the responsibility for food and drinks will fall upon him, his cohost can help by engaging his business associates and helping spouses and dates become acquainted.

A WORD OF CAUTION

Since home entertaining merges your business and social lives, exert caution when undertaking it. If, as an upper management executive, you socialize regularly with your staff, there is a chance that you may weaken your position of authority, making it difficult to reprimand or fire someone, or to pass over someone for a raise or a promotion. If you socialize with your boss, and your coworkers do not, you may create resentment among the rest of the staff and be accused of deliberately currying favor. Home entertainment on a regular basis should be confined to peers or clients who have become friends. The occasional home party may include anyone in the office.

ENTERTAINING THE BOSS

Inviting the boss to lunch or dinner can be a tricky proposition. You may invite a coworker, a client, a prospective client, a peer from another company, and—from time to time—your secretary or assistant, to breakfast, lunch, or dinner during the business week. If you are the boss, you may invite any members of your staff and colleagues from another company. But it's not a good idea to invite a superior to a restaurant during the business day. There are some rare exceptions, such as if you've worked with your boss for many years, or are old friends who knew each other before you worked together.

If someone in a superior position invites you or you and your spouse or live-in partner to a *social* occasion, however, you are expected to return the invitation in some way. The following are a few guidelines that may lessen the dilemma:

• In general, an invitation extended in person is okay for coworkers, but you might want to send your boss a written invitation. Write the invitation to your boss and his or her spouse.

• If you call your boss "Mr." or "Ms." at the office, don't suddenly switch to "Bob" or "Betty" either in the invitation or as you speak during the evening—that is, unless our boss suggests it. If you call your boss by title and last name, your spouse should follow suit. If you and your spouse address your boss by title and last name, you should both address his or her spouse similarly.

• You may find it easier to entertain your boss if you include a few other guests. Select people with similar interests.

• You need not reciprocate your boss's invitation in kind. For instance, you may repay a fancy dinner at a restaurant with a simple buffet dinner in your home.

• Finally, don't put on airs when you entertain the boss. Act as you normally act; entertain as you normally entertain. Do not hire special help unless you ordinarily do; do not serve a hard-to-carve roast unless you can handle it. In other words, be yourself and be comfortable. Being gracious and interested will impress the boss far more than outdoing yourself in a way that he, above all, knows you cannot afford.

WEDDINGS

Keep in mind that weddings should never be used as an opportunity to pay off business obligations or to sell or promote a business deal. Some business executives do use the occasion of a large wedding to entertain clients, prospective clients, and business associates. First, if the wedding is that of a son or daughter, do so only with his or her approval—even if you are paying for the entire wedding. Second, be careful not to slight anyone by failure to extend an invitation. Naturally, you would invite business associates who are also friends without having to invite the entire department or your complete client list.

OFFICE PARTIES

INVITATIONS

Invitations to office parties are more informal than those for social affairs. The host may send a memo on paper or by e-mail to each staff member. It might read something like: "The graphic services department will celebrate a good year and a merry Christmas on Friday, December 23, in the office. All work stops at 3:30 P.M. sharp for cocktails and a buffet. I look forward to celebrating with you." When an office party is held in a restaurant rather than in the office, invitations may sometimes be more formal—on cards, handwritten for small groups, printed for large ones.

Details of party arrangements—generally, the food and drinks—are often delegated to staff members. Some offices plan entertainment, whether music, gift-giving, or a sports-related activity.

THE HOLIDAY PARTY

A holiday party held during the Christmas season is usually hosted by the company. In a larger company, the heads of individual departments may host parties for their own staffs. If the department head is away or eschews holding parties, a lower-level executive may host the party instead. In rare cases, the staff throws its own party.

Spouses and dates may or may not be invited. At office parties held at a restaurant, the host generally stands by the door and greets each staff member upon arrival. In the office the host circulates, shaking hands and greeting the staff with a personal word of thanks.

OFFICE PARTY DRESS

At a party held in the workplace, both men and women generally just show up in the clothes they have worn all day. Or, they may have brought along a glittery top to change into or worn fancier dress than usual that morning in anticipation of the event. Although overdressing—not to mention underdressing—is generally out of place, many women like to dress up their office wear with jewelry or other accessories.

At an office party held outside the office, both men and women may properly change from work clothes into dress clothes. Still, because it is a business affair, overly dressy or revealing clothing is in poor taste.

RETURNING AN INVITATION

Business invitations need not be returned in the same way that social invitations must be. You do not return a business lunch or dinner invitation from your boss, but you do return, in some form, a social invitation. If, as a client, a salesperson or supplier invites you or entertains you, you are not expected to repay the business lunch or dinner, although you certainly may if you have continuing business together. Neither are you expected to repay a social invitation where you, as a client, have been entertained, even if the invitation has included your spouse or your entire family. You are, however, expected to return social invitations from coworkers and other business associates, whether they have extended a hand of friendship to cement a business relationship or simply because you enjoy one another's company outside the office.

THANK-YOU GIFTS AND NOTES

When you have been entertained for a business-related occasion that crosses from business to social— whether at a dinner, an evening out with your spouse, a weekend house party at the home of an employer, or as guest of honor at an office party—a thank-you note is in order. When you are one of many guests at an office party or a restaurant where you share a meal in the ordinary course of business, a verbal thanks at the end of the occasion is sufficient. While it is never wrong to write a thank-you note, you may reiterate your thanks in your next business correspondence in place of a separate note.

When the occasion is a social one, your thank-you note should be addressed to your host and his or her spouse and sent to their home. Social thank-you notes are handwritten on informal or personal stationery.

Business-occasion thank-you notes come in sev-eral varieties. If your company honors you with a dinner celebrating your twenty-five years with the firm, for example, a handwritten note on personal stationery is called for, addressed to your immediate boss, and to the president of the company if he or she attended the gathering.

If you, as the client, have been a lunch guest, a thank-you note is called for. But if you speak to your host often, a verbal thanks is sufficient. If you are the lunch guest of a client you see regularly, a separate note of thanks is not necessary. You would, instead, mention your thanks for the lunch in your next letter.

When a business lunch is a first meeting or an infrequent one, a short note is in order, whether typed by your secretary on business letterhead or handwritten by you.

CHAPTER 10

CHILDREN'S PARTIES

It's a proven fact that children can be taught from an early age to be gracious hosts and hostesses. Impress upon your own kids the importance of making guests feel comfortable and welcome in your home.

Children who are guests need help, too. Younger children need to know what to say when they are served a food they don't like, as well as what to do when a friend is bossy, overbearing, or boring. Older children need to be taught the same skills, as well as all the rules of courtesy, respect for others and their property, and safety when in circumstances away from home.

The bottom line regarding children's parties is that children simply enjoy being together, and the younger they are, the less formal or elaborate or expensive the entertainment they need.

PLANNING THE PARTY

Your child will get so much more enjoyment out of the party if he or she is an active participant in the party planning.

If you are having the party at home, make sure you have more activities planned than you need. Children often race from one game to another, and you may end up having to come up with something more to do on the spot.

When planning activities, take time into consideration. Most children's parties last on average two hours. Plot out the party's schedule with time frames for each activity.

If you plan to send invitations, mail them out at least two weeks in advance.

Don't forget to appoint a designated camera operator. Ask a friend, relative, or another parent to man the camera or camcorder.

USING A THEME

A party needs no theme to be a success; it's fun, however, to design a party around a child's favorite activity, fairy tale, movie, cartoon, or toy. Everything, from the food to the decor to the party dress, can revolve around the theme.

Plan, for example, an arts and crafts party. Best for children over five and under twelve, an arts and crafts party—where the kids are involved in creating something fun and original—can be a treat. Try bead-making, finger-painting, or making video movies.

Or let music be your theme. Invite a musician or two who has a repertoire of children's tunes.

Food preparation can also be a party theme. Cookie decorating and pizza making are fun activities; or, you could give guests the fixings to build their own banana splits or ice cream sundaes.

PARTY REFRESHMENTS

Children prefer simple, comforting fare, such as hamburgers, pizza, or fried chicken. Stick with the tried-and-true.

Avoid potentially chokable foods when entertaining young children; stay away from nuts, popcorn, even hot dogs.

Parents who monitor their children's intake of sugar may either have to compromise a bit on party day, be there to keep sweets out of their kids' hands, or refuse the invitation altogether. If your child has a physical problem or is allergic to a certain food, explain that to the mother of the hosting child before the party.

If you're the host, keep sweets and caffeinated soft drinks to a manageable level.

Avoid breakable cookwear and serving wear such as china and glass. Serve foods on paper plates and beverages in plastic glasses.

PARTY FAVORS

Party favors are generally given to guests as they leave the party. A colorful bag of inexpensive toys, crayons, or candy treats is a nice gesture.

Take a Polaroid of each child with the little host or hostess and include it in the party favors bag at the end of the party.

BIRTHDAY PARTIES

The younger the child, the shorter, smaller, and simpler the party.

The worst custom in some communities is parental competition over children's birthday parties and gifts. Gifts may or not be part of the proceedings.

Some parents don't let their children open their gifts until everyone has gone home, partly because they want to keep all duplicates intact so they can return or exchange them. There are several compelling reasons, however, to have children open their gifts in front of their friends. First, it is one of the moments of the party where the birthday child is in the limelight. Second, other children are often excited about the gift they are giving and are anxious to see him or her open it and express pleasure. Third, it is an opportunity for children to use their best manners by thanking their friends—and they should be told ahead of time to graciously thank the person who gave a duplicate gift or a peculiar one.

When the gift is opened and the donor is thanked personally at the time of the opening, a thank-you note is not necessary—although writing notes is a habit well worth teaching at an early age. If the gifts are opened later, the birthday child should definitely write a personal note to every giver, mentioning the gift by name.

SLEEPOVERS

When a child or teenager goes to spend a long weekend with friends, the same basic rules apply as do for adults. House rules must be respected. When your child is hosting a sleepover, you have every right to enforce these rules, and your children's guests are expected to honor your wishes.

The visitor should take a gift, preferably a "house" present rather than a "hostess" present. A tin of cookies, a plant, a movie on video—anything that can be enjoyed by the whole family—are all good choices.

If your child is a houseguest-to-be, remind him before going to be polite and helpful—not only to his friend, but to his friend's parents and siblings. Remind him to pick up after himself, to make his bed, and to leave the bathroom clean. He should *not* leave socks, shoes, and sweaters, for example, lying around the house. Even though the menus may not offer his favorite foods, he should try everything and keep his feelings to himself if he is disappointed. He must, of course, obey any household rules laid down by his friend's parents.

It is always a nice touch to have your teenager write a thank-you letter to his friend's mother. This is not at all necessary for the casual sleepover at a friend's house on a Friday or Saturday night; a verbal thanks in the morning will suffice—but a note is still a good idea.

PARTIES OUTSIDE THE HOME

A popular treat for kids is a party in a fun venue outside the home, whether a roller-skating rink, a bowling alley, or a sports complex. If you're the host, you'll need to make the necessary arrangements in advance. First, get a head count and make sure the rink or alley will be able to accommodate your group.

You may need to order food ahead of time, or at least determine what foods are available.

If you are hosting a party for kids under twelve years old, make sure you have a sufficient number of adults to supervise the group.

If you are the host, it is your responsibility to pay for the group's tickets, any rented shoes or skates, and food. (Call ahead to check on special group rates.)

Make sure that each child has reliable transportation to and from the party site; give parents a detailed list containing the time and address.

CHAPTER 11

THEME PARTIES

Planning a party around a theme—whether a card game, gourmet cooking, a special event, or simply a creative concept—can be as entertaining as the party itself. Make your occasion a memorable one by plotting all the details around a common theme.

CARD PARTIES

In giving a card party, whether of two tables or of ten, the first thing to do is to plan the pairings carefully. The tables may all be different—one with good players, another with beginners; one where the stakes are high, another where they play for nothing—but do your best to put those who play approximately the same kind of game at the same table.

Have a fresh pack of cards on each table and freshly sharpened pencils beside score pads. Make sure that each table is comfortably lighted. Poorly placed light that is reflected from the shiny surface of the cards is just as bad as darkness—and can make hearts and diamonds indistinguishable from spades and clubs. If you have any doubt about the light, sit in each place, hold the cards in your hands, lay a few on the table, and see for yourself.

The kinds of refreshments you offer your card-playing guests depend on the time of day. While tea sandwiches and petit fours accompanied by tea or coffee are suitable for a 4:00 P.M. game, they don't satisfy at an evening gathering.

A dessert card party is a happy compromise for the hostess who feels that she cannot provide a full luncheon or dinner for her guests.

If it is customary in your community to play for prizes, select a first prize for the highest score made by a woman and a first prize for the highest score made by a man. Sometimes a second prize is given. All prizes should be wrapped before being presented.

BOOK OR READING GROUPS

Among the most popular entertainments these days are book clubs, in which friends or acquaintances who love to read form a group that meets once a month for discussion. Often the meetings include food and drinks. The convenience of the members determines the hour, and the meeting place is usually rotated among the members.

Refreshments are generally served after the activity of the meeting. The host or hostess may want to provide snacks or cookies and coffee during the book discussion.

GOURMET COOKING CLUBS

An equally popular entertainment is the formation of

gourmet or cooking clubs, where the members of the group—generally from six to twelve people—cook meals for one another. Often, a theme is selected, such as a Mexican or Thai cuisine or favorite comfort foods, and everyone in the club makes a dish that reflects that theme. The venue is held at a different member's home each time the group meets, and the host generally is responsible for sodas, coffee, tea, mixers, condiments, and the table setting. Wine tastings are often a part of the meal. A gourmet club party is different from other types of entertaining in that it is a good place to boldly try out new recipes.

TV PARTIES

The television is such an integral part of modern life that parties are often planned around a favorite program or an annual televised event. Academy Award parties, for example, are an excuse for guests to wear campy evening wear and elaborate makeup. Super Bowl and Olympics parties are extremely popular, and are often accompanied by cold beer and a big stew pot of something hearty. The rules of TV parties are determined by the host or hostess, with basic thoughtfulness and concern for guests' comfort being the primary requisite.

POOL PARTIES

As anyone who owns one can tell you, the luxury of a

swimming pool in the backyard has obligations attached beyond that of pool upkeep. To a cool pool flocks swimmers, and the pool owner often ends up entertaining friends and neighbors all summer long.

Pools are great fun to have, but you must stand firm in some ways, or thoughtless neighbors will immediately impose on you. One solution to the problem of neighborhood children and adults dropping in to swim is to install a small flagpole at the gate to the pool. Inform friends and neighbors that they are invited to swim whenever the flag is raised. It will also mean that an adult will be there to supervise. When you have guests, or simply want the pool to yourselves, keep the flag down—and the neighborhood will know the pool is off limits.

If you are invited to enjoy a friend's pool, you should:

BRING YOUR OWN TOWELS. Most hosts and hostesses keep a supply on hand, as well as an extra swimsuit or two, but the work of laundering and providing towels for guests can be extensive.

BRING YOUR OWN BEVERAGES AND SNACKS. Any pool owner who finds that he is providing refreshments as well as swimming privileges to the neighborhood on a regular basis should tell his guests that he cannot go on providing snacks and drinks. Return the hospitality of a pool-owning friend by bringing sandwiches for the group and offering to buy soft drinks, beer, or iced tea.

HELP SUPERVISE WHEN YOUR CHILDREN ARE INVITED OVER TO SWIM. Children's pool parties—even those of teens—should have adult supervision. Water accidents do happen, and few children are equipped to handle them competently.

HOLIDAY OPEN HOUSE

An open house is literally what the name implies. The door is open to all those invited at any time between the hours stated on the invitation. Most open houses these days are held to celebrate a holiday. A particularly popular holiday for an open house is Christmas.

Personal invitations are generally sent out on informal or commercial cards bought for the occasion. Most holiday open houses don't request an RSVP—if anything, invitations may include a "Regrets only" notation.

Because most holiday cocktail parties and open houses offer staggered times so guests can come and go, guests at open houses generally stay no more than an hour.

A holiday open house is likely to be decorated with all the trimmings of the season; the food also follows a holiday theme. Eggnog, grog, or wassail are traditional drinks at a Christmas open house, and a bowl of eggnog may be surrounded by sprigs of seasonal greenery. A platter of Christmas cookies is a holiday party staple.

BYOB AND BYOF PARTIES

Bring-your-own-beverage parties are usually planned by a group that wants the costs of a social event to be shared, or by people who are on a tight budget and can't possibly entertain a group of friends if they have to provide *all* the refreshments. In the latter case, friends are often called upon to provide the liquid refreshment while the host or hostess provides the food, mixers, and soft drinks. In a written invitation, all that is necessary is a "BYOB" in the corner of the invitation.

Bring-your-own-food, or potluck, parties are given for much the same reasons as BYOB parties. The hosts want to bring friends together and have a good time, but often can't afford to do it all without help. In other instances, potluck parties are held not for economic reasons but simply because it's fun for all involved to actively participate.

THE GREAT OUTDOORS: BARBECUES AND PICNICS

THE BARBECUE

The backyard barbecue one of the most delightful and quintessentially all-American ways to entertain informally. And because it is so informal, a barbecue is one of the easiest parties to put on.

Planning a Barbecue

Since the setting is outside, disposable plates, cups, and utensils are appropriate. Provide enough tables and chairs for everyone, or at least comfortable places to sit.

For an evening barbecue, make sure the chef has enough light to see what he is cooking and the guests to be able to maneuver easily. Floodlights directed into the trees give a beautiful effect, as do colorful Japanese paper lanterns or candles placed in hurricane lamps. Citronella candles are an excellent idea for a summer night, since they help keep insects away.

The Barbecue Menu

A barbecue menu features a main dish, whether meat, fish, vegetables, or fowl, prepared on the grill. Some people prefer to serve dishes that can be eaten as finger food, such as hamburgers or barbecued ribs.

Since barbecue food is generally hearty and rib-sticking, elaborate hors d'oeuvres are not necessary. A few bowls of nuts or potato chips, crudités, and dips are sufficient.

If you choose to serve steak, be prepared with knives and sturdy plastic plates or china—it is hard to cut steak on flimsy paper plates without tearing the plate.

If you're serving hamburgers, hot dogs, or steak, load up a side table with a variety of condiments, such as ketchup, mustard, relish, and steak sauce.

Prepare side dishes, such as potato salad, coleslaw, or baked beans, in advance and keep them refrigerated until you're ready to serve them.

Beer, soft drinks, and wine all go well with the informality of a barbecue. In hot weather, iced tea, iced coffee, and icy sangria are delicious. Keep pots of coffee hot on the grill for serving either during or after the meal.

THE PICNIC

Picnics are perfect entertainments for celebrations involving large groups of people, family reunions, or simply enjoying a beautiful outdoor venue. The idea behind picnics is that most of the food is prepared at home and then moved to an outdoor setting, often a pretty park, a beach, or a designated picnic site where picnic tables and grilling facilities are located. The trick is making sure your moveable feast undergoes a smooth transition. Here are a few general directions for avid picnickers.

Planning a Picnic

You can arrange a group picnic, where you offer to bring the main dish and have each guest contribute a dish, condiments, drinks, or paper goods. Or have each person or family bring its own food to cook over a community fire. This sort of picnic is especially fine when children are included, as parents know best what their young ones prefer to eat.

Consider your picnic location carefully. If the

weather is hot, look for a shady spot; if the wind is blustery, look for a natural wind barrier. Look for a place with picnic tables if the ground is too uncomfortable to lay down a blanket. Consider whether insects will be a problem.

Make sure that you serve the food without too much delay—preferably within an hour of the guests' arrival (unless you have planned a specific activity beforehand).

If the guest list includes several elderly or infirm individuals, make sure there are plenty of folding chairs or ask guests to bring extra blankets.

The Picnic Menu

You can either prepare all of your picnic food beforehand—taking only things that are ready to serve, such as sandwiches, cold chicken, or a pasta salad—or you can bring a few prepared foods and cook the rest on a grill.

The simplest type of picnic is a continental one— as if straight from the farms of Europe. It may consist of a loaf of bread, a piece of cheese, a hard salami or paté, marinated olives, and a bottle of wine. Use these classic picnic foods as a base, and add your own variations: fresh tomatoes, basil, and mozzarella sandwiches, for example, or a cold olive and sun-dried tomato pasta.

Summertime lends itself well to an outdoor feast of seasonal fresh foods. Cold boiled lobster or steamed shrimp accompanied by coleslaw, a fresh

corn salad, and fresh summer berries make a meal
that is truly fit for a king. Grilled meat or fish, whole
potatoes or corn wrapped in foil and roasted in the
coals, and a mixed green salad make a perfect meal.
Top it off with cold sliced watermelon or hand-
cranked homemade ice cream.

Plates for a picnic that includes hot foods should
be more substantial than uncoated paper. You can use
plastic or enameled ones, even though they must be
taken home to be washed.

Plastic bowls or cups for chowder are more
leakproof and easier to hold than paper cups. As long
as you are bringing the utensils for this type of meal,
there is no reason not to accompany your main dish
with a salad already mixed in a big bowl and breads
kept warm by several layers of foil wrapping.

Don't forget to pack coffee or tea in a thermos
and have plenty of cold beverages to drink in hot
weather. Stock up on freezer packs to keep foods cool
on summer days. This also helps prevent food
spoilage, a warm-weather hazard when food is not
kept cold enough.

No matter where your picnic has taken place, be
sure not only to tidy up before you leave, but to be
careful not to throw trash carelessly aside during the
festivities. Most important of all, *never* leave a fire
without being absolutely certain that it is out. In the
woods water may be poured on the logs until there is
no sign of steam; or, if you have a shovel or other
means of lifting them, embers may be put out and

then buried. On the beach a fire should also be put out with water. *Never* cover the coals with sand until they are completely cool, as they will retain the heat for hours, and someone walking by with bare feet, unable to see the remains of the fire, may step on the hot sand and receive a terrible burn.

Tailgate Picnics

The origin of the tailgate picnic lies in the station wagons of old, the ones with the big, heavy tailgates that were lowered and used as a table for food and fixings, generally in the parking lot outside a football stadium or other sports site. These days it is not necessary to have a tailgate to have a tailgate party. Some people use the back of a sports utility vehicle; others simply bring along a folding table. The only other piece of equipment you may need is a grill. You don't even need a football game to enjoy a delightful picnic with friends; you can tailgate before a concert, for example, or during a day at the races.

PARTIES WITH A TWIST

Half the fun of a party, for many people, is in the planning. Some people just have a knack for creative party giving. If you're tired of the same old "Cocktails at 6:00," here are a few ideas for something new and different.

MURDER MYSTERY

Many party planners specialize in complete murder-mystery dinners, where guests try to solve a murder mystery much as the weekend houseguests in Agatha Christie's mystery books would do. A less expensive way to go is to buy a murder-mystery party kit, available in game or toy stores.

COME AS YOU ARE

This is a theme that can be easily expanded upon: Try a Come-As-You-Wish-You-Were party, a Come-As-Your-Favorite-Hero party, a Come-As-Your-Favorite-Villain party, a Come-As-Your-Favorite-Movie-Star party, and on and on.

TIME WARP

Everyone is invited to come dressed in the style of a designated decade, the music of that decade is played, and the food of that decade is served. These are especially fun when celebrating a big birthday for someone who was born or came of age in a particular decade.

MAD HATTER

Everyone invited to this party wears a goofy or unique and original hat.

PARTY GAMES AND MUSICAL
ENTERTAINMENT

Often, a host or hostess has planned games or entertainment for the evening. It may simply be music, a
mystery game, charades, or board games. It is incumbent upon guests to be sporting about it, no matter
how silly they think the idea.

If the entertainment consists of background
music during cocktails and dinner, the host should
ensure that it is unobtrusive. That means it should
generally be instrumental rather than vocal and at a
relaxed tempo. It should be at background level, not
loud, so that it doesn't interfere with quiet conversation. Good choices include piano arrangements and
classical recordings performed by ensemble groups.

CHAPTER 12

LAST-MINUTE ENTERTAINING

TAKE-OUT ENTERTAINING

What would Emily Post think of entertaining with take-out food? She would probably approve and consider it a perfectly fine way to enjoy the company of friends in a casual setting. Today, more and more people have less and less time to prepare elaborate meals. The important issue is that friends have an opportunity to visit with one another.

Take-out entertaining can take many forms. Ordering pizzas or Chinese dishes for a group is one version. Another is blending takeout with a potluck meal, with the host making a big main dish, such as spaghetti or chili, and each guest bringing a take-out dish from a different source to make a complete meal. One guest may bring the bread from a bakery, for example, another guest would bring pastries, and another guest would bring a salad.

Takeout these days doesn't have to be relegated to pizza or hamburgers. Gourmet food stores offer delicious and elaborate dishes to go. Delis will make huge sliced meat and salad platters. Even mail-order takeout is taking off: Order out and a day later you'll have fresh Florida stone crabs, Vermont hickory-smoked bacon, or Scottish salmon delivered to your door.

Any way you cut it, take-out entertaining is generally a casual affair. So don't fret over correct table settings; in fact, sturdy paper plates, festive paper napkins, and plastic utensils are the tools of choice. As the host or hostess, however, you always want to make your guests feel taken care of and comfortable. That means you should greet your guests enthusiastically, let them serve themselves first, enjoy their company, and give them a warm send-off at the end of the party.

TIPS FOR QUICK MEALS

The busy cook doesn't have to rely on preprocessed convenience foods—which are often high in salt, fat, and nonnutritious filler—to prepare quick, delicious meals. The advantage: modern tools and cooking methods that make preparing fresh, nutritious foods a snap. The following are a few tips on preparing complete meals in no time.

• Use your microwave. These timesaving appliances let you (among other things) bake potatoes in no time, quickly heat up leftovers, wilt spinach for spinach salad, cook bacon fast (and with less fat), rapidly thaw frozen foods, and toast nuts.

• Invest in a food processor and a blender.

• Grill whenever you can.

• Freeze pie crusts and puff pastries for quick quiches and pies.

• Don't throw out day-old rice or pasta. For example, you can sauté leftover linguini with olive oil, garlic, sun-dried tomatoes, and olives for a filling meal.

• Keep cold cuts and sliced cheeses on hand for quickie make-your-own sandwiches. Your sandwich spread could include jars of grilled marinated peppers, sun-dried tomatoes, and oil-cured olives, all of which have a long shelf life. Always refrigerate after opening, however.

• Always have eggs in your fridge. One of the easiest and most elegant dishes you can whip up is an omelet. Fill with whatever leftover meats and vegetables you have on hand.

• Keep canned meat broths and bouillon cubes on hand; many recipes call for the addition of stocks and broths, and cooking them takes time.

• Stock up on fresh items when they are in season and freeze the overage. If you find a good deal on fresh shrimp in August, for example, buy in bulk and freeze in one-pound containers what you don't use.

• Whenever you're faced with a surplus of food— a neighbor with a garden drops off ten pounds of tomatoes, for example—it's a smart idea to make a big pot of something, whether tomato sauce, vegetable soup, or chili con carne. Even smarter: When preparing a meal, make more than you need and freeze the surplus. Anytime you have a last-minute guest or your special dinner flopped, simply thaw the frozen food for a last-minute home-cooked treat. Casseroles, pasta dishes, soups, and stews will keep in the freezer from six to twelve months.

• Anytime you can, freeze leftover meat and vegetable stocks. One good way to do this is to set aside an ice-cube tray, pour cooled stock into the tray, and freeze. When you need some chicken stock, for example, simply pop out a cube or two to drop into a dish for richer flavor.

• Be on the lookout for sales at your local grocery so that you can buy in bulk. Don't forget to have a supply of beverages and napkins on hand. Here are some foods to have around that you can arrange in minutes to serve as appetizers:

• jars of salsa
• jars or cans of nuts
• tins of minced clams, pâté, and smoked oysters
• dried soup mixes (combine with sour cream to make great dips)
• bean dip
• olive oil and red wine vinegar
• jars of marinated artichokes
• jars of sun-dried tomatoes
• chips, crackers, and microwave popcorn
• jams and jellies
• anchovies and anchovy paste
• jars of marinated sweet peppers

CHAPTER 13

PARTIES WITH CHILDREN AND PETS

FOR THE HOST

Children and pets alter the tone of a party. Simply by their nature, kids and pets bring an informality to the party, and the hostess relinquishes some measure of control over the proceedings. If you as a host are inviting a couple to a dinner party but don't want their children to come, simply call and say, "Do you think you could get a sitter for Saturday night so that you and Jim could come to dinner?"

If, however, you do include your friends' child on a dinner-party invitation, and you don't have young children living at home, it's a smart idea to childproof the premises before an expected visit from little ones. Remove anything breakable or sharp that is within easy reach. Shut the doors to rooms you consider off-limits, and see that doors to cellar steps and low windows are tightly closed. Then, when safety precautions are taken care of, check the supply of recreational materials. A basket or sack of simple toys—coloring books, blocks, and comic books—or a sampling of children's videotapes goes a long way toward making the visit enjoyable for both parent and host. And a supply of cookies and milk or soft drinks fits the bill when the novelty of the toys wears off.

If the child invited to your home proves to be ill-mannered, you have every right to correct him. But you should only reproach him for breaking house rules, not for displaying poor personal behavior. You can tell him that in your house you don't sing at the table or wear hats, but you should not correct his (admittedly poor) personal behavior. Any word about your expectations—"In our house, it's hats off!"—should be mentioned, preferably in private.

FOR THE GUESTS

The standard is: Unless your children—or pets—are specifically invited, leave them at home when you visit friends or attend a social gathering. Often, however, it is difficult for couples with young children, for example, or people who are new in town or who can't afford a baby-sitter, to get away. In those cases, it's perfectly all right to ask the host politely whether or not the kids can come, too.

If the answer is yes, you as parents can ensure that your children will be welcome guests in many ways. Toddlers should not be taken on visits until they learn the meaning of no. Don't let your child run around unsupervised, or eat and drink wherever he wants—a host is perfectly within her rights to set limits and to verbally enforce them. Bring a bag of favorite toys to keep your child occupied. And, with the knowledge that young children generally have short attention spans, set a time limit for the visit. End the visit before that limit is reached.

If your child is a guest among adults at a dinner party, help her out ahead of time. Picky eaters should be taught that it is extremely rude to turn up their noses when offered something they don't like. It not only displays bad manners, but also hurts the feelings of the host. Tell your child to say instead, "No, thank you," and teach her how to say "I'd like a peanut butter and jelly sandwich, please" rather than shrugging or saying, "I don't know" when offered a choice. Remind her of some of the things that comprise good table manners so that she can be just as proud as you are of her skills.

When small children—whether your own or your guests'—are included in your dinner plans, it's perfectly correct to let them be excused from the table earlier than the adults, if they please. Have some activities available to occupy them while the adults are still eating; a video is a smart, relatively sedate choice. Avoid any rowdy after-dinner games guaranteed to send your guests' children home all worked up.

PARTY PETS

Even if your pet is beautifully behaved, if it is not invited to a social event you should leave it at home. Unless you know that the person you are visiting loves animals, never just show up with a pet or ask whether you may bring a pet along on a visit. If they are not enthusiastic about your request, you have put them in a difficult position. If they make the suggestion on their own, naturally your pet may go. Be sure, before you accept on its behalf, that its behavior will be exemplary.

If, on the other hand, you are a guest in the home of people who own pets, how do you protest without appearing rude when the family cat jumps on your lap? Remember: As a guest, you need never be subjected to animals that are not perfectly behaved or that expose you to allergens. Simply remain pleasant and ask whether the animal can be put in another room. A good host will automatically monitor the situation to make sure his cat or dog doesn't bother the guest.

CHAPTER 14

HOUSEGUESTS

Having guests stay at your home for a weekend or even longer is an especially hospitable gesture, but one that can test even the closest relationships. Whether you make your invitation over the phone or in a handwritten note, communicate to your houseguests clearly. State the dates and times the invitation covers, and include your plans so that your guests will know how to prepare. If you are having a formal dinner party during your houseguests' visit, let them know ahead of time so that they bring appropriate clothing. The same is true if you are planning a golf or boating trip, or a swimming day at the beach.

Communicate *during* the visit, as well. Show guests not only where their room, bathroom, towels, and other items are, but also where the refrigerator is. They should be made to feel comfortable helping themselves to snacks or beverages.

Finally, when good friends are visiting, don't be afraid to ask them to help, and don't, in your anxiety to be sure guests relax and have a good time, refuse all of their offers. Most guests sincerely want to help and feel uncomfortable if constantly rebuffed or if left to sit while you do all the work.

THE HOUSEGUEST'S GUIDEBOOK

It's of primary importance for houseguests to tell the hosts precisely when they are arriving *and* when they are leaving. If your host is expecting you to stay through Sunday evening, stay through Sunday evening. Don't plan at the last minute to leave after breakfast, because your host most likely has planned two more meals or may have refused another invitation to be with you. The following are some words of advice for houseguests.

Never ask if you may bring a pet along on a visit. Animal lovers they may be, but your weekend hosts probably do not want a strange dog on the premises—one who may or may not get along with their dog and whose manners may be found wanting. Your request puts the host in a difficult position. If, however, you simply cannot travel without your pet, thank your host and explain that you'll have to refuse as you don't travel without your pet. If your hostess then suggests that you bring it along, you may.

If your pet is invited, you need to make sure that it behaves. If, on your weekend visit to someone else's home, you introduce a pet who is not house-trained, who chews things, or who freely lounges on furniture or laps, you risk damaging your relationship with your hosts. Do make sure to clean up after your pet and offer to repair or replace any broken or chewed items.

It is not only courteous but obligatory to give your host or hostess a gift—and, if the household contains children, to take presents to them. Give your gift to your hostess as soon as you arrive. If you send it later, be sure to do it as soon as possible. Another option is to find the perfect hostess gift while you are visiting.

Just as it is incumbent upon you to share your arrival and departure plans with your hostess, it is important to let her know if you have other plans. If, for example, she lives in the same town as another friend with whom you would like to visit, say so in advance. Determine the best day and time for you to make your visit, and make sure it doesn't disrupt your host's schedule. If you don't communicate this ahead of time and simply announce that you are leaving for a few hours in the middle of your visit, you may be spoiling an activity organized for your pleasure. Knowing ahead that you will be occupied for a period of time gives her the opportunity to do some personal errands.

If you run into other friends in the area and they invite you and your hosts over for a swim or to play tennis, you should never accept the invitation without checking with your hostess beforehand.

If you plan to take your host and hostess out to dinner one evening during a stay of three days or more, discuss this ahead of time rather than surprising them at the last minute. Again, letting them know ahead of time enables them to plan appropriately for your visit. Otherwise your hostess may already have planned and prepared a special meal at home.

If your hostess is a good friend, offer to bring food for an evening's meal. Your hostess will probably be happy to accept such an offer. On an informal weekend, guests feel more comfortable if they can contribute.

Both weekend guest and hostess need time apart from one another. Let your hostess know that you jog an hour every day unless there is something you can do with her instead. This gives her the opportunity to get some of her own things done.

Be adaptable. You must always be ready for anything—or nothing. If the plan is to picnic—and you can't bear picnics—graciously and enthusiastically soldier through the experience.

Remember that wise adage, "Neither a borrower nor a lender be." Try to take everything you need with you. But if you *must* borrow, return the article as soon as you can and in good shape. If you borrow a book from your hosts, don't dog-ear it by turning the corners of the pages down; find a piece of paper to use as a bookmark. Don't go home with a book you have started without your host's permission. If he does suggest that you take it home, return it promptly unless he tells you explicitly that he does not want it back.

WHEN THE HOUSEGUESTS ARE FAMILY

As a good hostess, you want all your houseguests to feel that while they are guests in your house they are part of the family. Sometimes, however, when actual family members visit, they forget that they are guests. It's not uncommon to find brothers, cousins, in-laws, nieces, and nephews sprawled all over the house and never lifting a

TELEPHONE CALLS MADE
BY HOUSEGUESTS

Many visitors forget to offer to pay for their calls. The definite rule is this: Should a houseguest be obliged to make a local call or two, he or she would not ordinarily offer payment for it, but it is absolutely required that every long-distance call be paid for. Moreover, this is the only way in which a houseguest can feel free to telephone as often as he or she may want to. The best solution: If you're a guest in someone's home, take along a calling card or telephone credit card, or access the operator and arrange to have calls billed to your home number. Another way the guest can pay is to call the operator as soon as the call is finished and ask, for example, for "the toll charge on 212-555-9121." The necessary amount should be left with a slip, giving the date and the number called. If it is a substantial amount, tax should be added. Or if a visitor has used the telephone a great deal during a long stay, the complete list of calls with the amounts of each and their total should be handed to the host or hostess and paid for when the houseguest leaves. No matter how wealthy the host may be, this debt should be paid.

One additional note: Houseguests should not answer the phone while visiting unless they ask, "Would you like me to answer?" or the hostess says, "My hands are all wet—would you take that call?" And, when a houseguest answers the phone, he should ask who is calling and offer to take a message.

finger to help. A sister may break house rules by eating on the living-room sofa, for example, or a mother-in-law may expect to be waited on hand and foot. In either case, you'll need to gently lay down the law.

Then there are the visits from family members who take over and disrupt the routine of the household. They meddle, advise, and contradict the wishes of the heads of the household. It's unlikely that he or she will have a lasting effect on the household routine—however, if you find yourself resenting this person's visits, it is perfectly fine to explain, in a gentle and nonaccusatory way, that while you know her intentions are good, sometimes her actions make you feel uncomfortable or resentful.

SKI WEEKENDS: A GUEST'S GUIDE

When invited to be someone's guest for a weekend of skiing, you are a houseguest, and as such will follow the guidelines for being a gracious houseguest. If you don't ski and have no desire to learn, simply say so. If, on the other hand, you do ski or would like to learn but have no equipment, you cannot expect your host to supply it. Your host is providing lodging and hospitality but is certainly not obliged to pay the considerable costs associated with skiing for his houseguests. Either rent the equipment from a store or ask your host if rentals are available at the slopes. Insist on paying for your own rentals as well as the cost of your lift tickets.

PART III

PARTY PARTICULARS

CHAPTER 15

INTRODUCTIONS AND CONVERSATIONS

INTRODUCTIONS: THE BASICS

There are three basic guidelines regarding introductions:

In social situations, a man is introduced to a woman.
> *"Mrs. Pullman, I'd like you to meet Mr. Havlin."*
> *"Janny, this is my cousin, John Vaccaro."*
> *"Mr. DeRuvo, may I introduce you to my mother, Mrs. Smithson?"*

In business, the order is based on rank, not gender. A young person is introduced to an older person.
> *"Dr. Josephson, I'd like you to meet my daughter, Lily Peterson."*
> *"Aunt Ruth, this is my roommate, Elizabeth Feeney."*

A less prominent person is introduced to a more important person. This last guideline can be complicated, since it may be difficult to determine who is more prominent. Here is a tip that may help in some circumstances: Members of your family, even though they may be more prominent, are introduced to the other person as a matter of courtesy.

"Mr. Connor, I'd like you to meet my stepfather, Governor Bradley."

"Mrs. Anselmi, this is my aunt, Professor Johnston."

The following are some general guidelines for making introductions.

Don't introduce people by their first names only. Always include a person's full name.

Avoid expressing your introduction as a command, such as: "Mr. Bonner, shake hands with Mr. Heath."

Avoid calling only one person "my friend" in an introduction, which implies that the other person is not your friend.

Do not repeat "Mr. Jones ... Mr. Smith. Mr. Smith ... Mr. Jones." To say each name once is enough.

PAYING ATTENTION

Just as you give a person who is being introduced to you your undivided attention, you should look a person to whom you are being introduced to in the eye and greet him or her cordially. Repeating the person's name—"Hello, Dr. Shine, it's certainly a pleasure to meet you"—is a technique that helps you remember the name and is a sign that you are, indeed, paying attention to the introduction. It's also very flattering to the person being introduced.

WHEN INCORRECTLY INTRODUCED

When someone is introducing a stranger to a number of people and consistently says the name wrong, the person being introduced should correct the one making the introduction as soon as he realizes it is not just a slip of the tongue. He should do so not with annoyance, but by making light of it. All he need say is, "I know it's confusing, but my name is 'Light,' not 'Bright,'" or "Actually, it's Frances, not Francesca."

If you are introduced by your correct name and someone immediately finds a diminutive or nickname for you, you may say, "Would you mind calling me Jeffrey? For some reason, I've never been called Jeff." If the other person insists on his own version, you may correct him one more time and, after that, just ignore his discourtesy the best that you can.

WHEN YOU DON'T USE FIRST NAMES

On occasion, you should not use first names in introductions. When meeting one of the following people, first names may not be used except when they request it.

A person of higher rank (a diplomat, a public official, or a professor, for example).

Professional people offering you their services (doctors, lawyers, and so on). In turn, they should not use your first name unless you request them to.

An older person, such as an adult to a child.

WHEN A GUEST IS UNKNOWN
TO THE HOSTESS

When you bring a guest whom no one knows to a party, remember to introduce him or her to everyone you possibly can. You don't have to make a grand tour of the room, but it is unfair to expect your hostess to look after *your* guest and have a stranger's name at the tip of her tongue all evening long.

WHEN TO RISE

Hosts and hostesses always rise to greet each arriving guest. Members of the host's family, including young people, also rise as a guest enters the room, although they do not all necessarily shake hands, with this exception: A youngster who is sitting and chatting with an adult need not rise as each new guest comes in. He should stand up instantly, however, if the guest is brought over to be introduced.

A woman does not stand when being introduced to someone at a distance. Nor need she rise when shaking hands with anyone, unless that person is much older, very prominent, someone she has wanted to meet for some time, or is someone with whom she wants to go on talking. In the first case, think before you leap. Some women would hardly feel complimented if a woman only a few years younger were to jump up for them.

In a social situation, a man should rise when a

woman comes into a room *for the first time* and remain standing until she is seated or leaves his vicinity. He does not jump up every time a hostess or another guest goes in and out. A husband rises for his wife when she comes in after they have been apart for a time. This is not a matter of manners, but simply of saying, "I'm glad to see you."

RECEIVING LINES

If the reception or party is a large celebration for a guest of honor, the hostess receives, standing with the special guest. As each guest approaches, the hostess says, "Mrs. Smith, this is my neighbor, Mrs. Johnson"; "Mr. Jones, our headmaster, Dr. Riley"; or simply "Mrs. Taylor, Mrs. Stokes." The guest of honor then offers his or her hand, and the other guest says, "How do you do?" or "I'm so glad to meet you," and moves on. A receiving line is never the place to conduct a prolonged conversation or say anything more than "How do you do," "I'm so pleased to meet you," or any other brief greeting.

When an invited guest has brought guests of her own to the reception, she precedes them in the line and introduces them to the hostess, who in turn introduces her and her guests to the guest of honor.

On formal occasions when (as a guest) you do not know any of the people in the line, nor could they be expected to know you, you introduce yourself formally. A woman might say, for example, "I am Janet

Smith" and, turning to her husband behind her, "and this is my husband, Charles Smith."

Introductions are always required when a guest of honor is presented to other guests. If you arrive after the receiving line has dispersed, you must introduce yourself; it is considered rude to attend a party given in honor of someone and fail to say "How do you do?" to him.

At a smaller, more casual party given for someone known to most of the people present, the guest of honor does not receive with the hostess but sits or stands in a convenient place so that everyone can go up and talk to him or her. Whether there is a receiving line or not, a woman introduces herself as "Janet Smith" and her husband as "my husband, Bob." If she is escorted by a person who is not her husband, she would introduce herself and say, "and this is Douglas Jones."

SPECIAL CASES

When introducing family members, it is not absolutely necessary to specify the relationship, but it is helpful to include an identifying phrase. This provides a conversational opening for strangers. Since you courteously give precedence to the other person when introducing a family member, the identifying phrase comes at the end of the introduction: "Mrs. Cottrell, I'd like you to meet my daughter, Deborah."

How does one introduce his or her live-in companion? Although you usually identify family members as such, you needn't identify boyfriends, girlfriends, or live-in companions with their relationship to you. Saying his or her name is sufficient.

Children, when introducing their parents, use first names depending on to whom they are making the introduction. One should always use the name that the newly introduced pair will use in talking to one another. If you are introducing your roommate to your father, he would, of course, call your father by the title "Mr." If you are introducing your roommate's father to your father, you would use your father's full name: "Mr. Davies, may I introduce my father, Franklin Palmer?"

- A child should be prepared to shake hands when introduced to adults who offer their hands to him or her.
- When a man is introduced to a woman, she smiles and says, "Hello" or "How do you do?" Traditionally speaking, in social situations, it is her place to offer her hand or not, as she chooses, but if he should extend his hand, she *must* give him hers. Nothing could be ruder than to ignore spontaneous friendliness.
- An older person extends his or her hand first to a younger one.
- A "more important" person offers his or her hand to a "less important" person.
- When you meet someone whose right arm or hand is missing or disabled, extend your right

HOW AND WHEN TO SHAKE HANDS

A handshake between two strangers can create
an immediate impression, ranging from warm
friendliness to instant irritation. A "boneless" hand
that feels like a limp glove is as big a turnoff as a
viselike grasp that temporarily paralyzes every finger.
The proper handshake is brief but firm and warm. It
should always be accompanied by a direct look into
the eyes of the person whose hand you are grasping.
Traditionally, shaking hands occurs when people are
introduced to one another or when they meet
acquaintances on the street, at a function or social
occasion, or in business situations. As in
introductions, there is a protocol for this form
of greeting.

hand even though he or she cannot shake hands
in the normal way. The disabled person will
appreciate that you have made no unnatural gesture to accommodate his or her problem. He or
she will respond by offering his or her left hand,
or by saying, "Please forgive me if I don't shake
hands, but I'm very glad to meet you."

- If you are disabled or are suffering an injury or
illness such as arthritis and it is impossible or
painful for you to shake hands, you shouldn't feel
you must. Simply say, as noted above, "I'm so
glad to meet you; please forgive me for not shaking hands. I have arthritis [or a sprained finger or
whatever the trouble may be]."

CONVERSATION: THE BASICS

Conversation should be a matter of equal give and take. For those inclined to run on at length, remember this simple rule: Stop, look, and listen. In conversation, "stop" means not to rush ahead without thinking; "look" means to pay attention to the expression of the person with whom you are talking; and "listen"— meaning exactly that—is the best advice possible, because everyone loves to talk to a sympathetic listener. Remember, though, that a sympathetic listener really listens.

Watch that wandering eye, too: There is nothing more frustrating than talking to someone who is constantly looking past your shoulder, as if he is bored to tears and is searching out a more interesting situation. It is particularly rude for a man or woman to bring a date to a party and then to scour the room for new conquests while in conversation with his or her date. Keep your eyes glued to whomever you are talking with, and you will have a friend for life.

Don't Panic

If you dread meeting strangers because you are afraid you won't be able to think of anything to say, relax and listen. Most conversational errors are committed not by those who talk too little but by those who talk too much.

Many people do have great difficulty in carrying

on a conversation. This terror is something like the terror felt by those who are learning to swim. It is not just the first stroke that overwhelms them, but the thought of all the strokes that must follow. The frightened talker doesn't hear a word that is said by others because he or she is trying so desperately to think of what to say next. So the practical rule for continuing a conversation is the same as that for swimming: Don't panic. Just take it one stroke (or word) at a time.

By careful listening to our own words and giving attention to the reactions of our listeners, we can discover our personal inadequacies. The burden of thinking before speaking is our own. It has been said that "I" is the smallest letter in the alphabet—don't make it the largest word in your vocabulary.

A CLEVER CONVERSATIONAL MIX

There are those who can recount the most mundane experience to a group of people and make everyone burst into laughter. But the storyteller who constantly tries to be funny is generally a bore, and the majority of us, if we wish to be considered attractive, are safer if we rely on sincerity, clarity, and an intelligent choice of conversational subject.

Guests who are interesting and amusing can set any party afire. On the other hand, a friend who is dear to you but who makes people's eyes glaze over as she goes on and on is not someone you can count on to make your gathering sparkle with humor. While you don't want your party to consist only of a roomful of divas duking it out, you also don't want it limited to a group of wallflowers. It's all in the mix.

TALKING TO NEW ACQUAINTANCES

When you find yourself next to a stranger at a party, introduce yourself right off the bat. It is not only good manners, but it is also a great help to your host or hostess. In introducing yourself, however, never start out with, "What is your name?" Doing so is simply too abrupt. Always start by giving your own name. "Hello. I'm Amelia Coppola," you may say, extending your hand if you wish. You can also add, "I'm a friend of Judy's." If this does not elicit a response other than "Hello," you may then say "And you are . . . ?" or "And what is your name?"

If you simply want to introduce yourself to someone, by all means, go ahead. It is fine to say, for instance, "Mrs. Simms, aren't you a friend of my mother's? I'm Jane Adams, Adelaide Pinkham's daughter."

DINNER-TABLE CONVERSATION

Although the turning of the table is no longer a dinner-party ritual, common courtesy dictates that you must at some time during dinner talk to both your neighbors. Today, conversation at the table often includes three or four people sitting near each other.

If, however, you notice that one of your neighbors is left with no one to talk to, common courtesy dictates that you should either include him in your conversation or turn at a break in your discussion to talk to him for a while.

Remember not to talk at length about yourself, but to listen to your neighbor's point of view, and avoid talking shop at great length to the exclusion of others seated near you.

Even if you imagine you have nothing in common with your neighbor and can't possibly converse, look around you. The food and wine always provide something worth talking about, as do the decor, the music, the fashions on display, and the people around you. It's all fodder for social interaction, no more complicated than connecting to people who are likely to have as much trepidation as you are in talking to strangers.

TEN CONVERSATIONAL BLUNDERS

A great number of comments, especially those that are extremely personal, should be off limits, whether you're conversing with new acquaintances or old friends. If your dinner partner wants to divulge a personal matter, he or she will initiate the conversation; it is never up to you to do so. The following are some things not to say when meeting new or old acquaintances.

1. "Why aren't you married? Why don't you have any children?"
2. "Why are you wearing that eye patch?"
3. "Are you tired? You look it." Or, even worse: "Have you had cosmetic surgery? You look so much better than you used to."
4. "How much did that cost?"
5. "You're dead wrong."
6. "How old are you? Ah, c'mon, you can tell me."
7. "That's pronounced *em-PIR.*"
8. ". . . you know, like, I mean . . ."
9. "As the President was telling me the other day . . ."
10. "I can see I'll have to simplify this for you."

CHAPTER 16

GIFT ETIQUETTE

GIFTS FOR THE HOST AND HOSTESS

It is certainly not necessary to present a host or hostess with an expensive, elaborate gift as a gesture of thanks. Remember: the more personal the gift, the more sincere and thoughtful—and the more thoughtful, the more meaningful to your host.

Always consider the nature of the occasion before you bring a gift. The gift you give to a weekend host should be grander than the one you take to a dinner party host. Some events—a cocktail party, say, or an open house—don't require a gift at all.

DINNER-PARTY GIFTS

Make sure you aren't simply giving the host one more thing to be responsible for. Flowers, wine, and food are all excellent gifts but can present their own set of problems. Flowers brought to a dinner party obligate an already busy hostess to find a vase and arrange them. Solve that by presenting your flowers in a vase. A small plant or floral arrangement eliminates the problem altogether.

Unless you have consulted with your dinner-party hostess about bringing a contribution toward the dinner, it's generally wise not to bring food as a gift. Doing so often puts the hostess on the spot. If you do bring a surprise gift of food, make it clear that the item is not intended for the meal being served (unless, of course, the host or hostess chooses to serve it).

The custom of taking wine as a gift to a small dinner party has become widespread. A bottle of wine is not too expensive or elaborate and can be shelved for later use by the host. Again, the host has no obligation to serve it with dinner.

Ordinarily, neither a gift nor a note sent later is necessary for a dinner-party invitation—especially if the party is a large one and you don't know your hosts well; your verbal thanks when you leave is enough. A phone call the next day—or even a note—to say how much you enjoyed the evening is always welcome.

The guest of honor at a dinner party should give a gift of thanks, perhaps flowers sent to the hostess before or on the day of the party.

GIFTS FOR A WEEKEND VISIT

Houseguests who stay a weekend or longer should always send or take a gift for their host and/or hostess.

The choice of gift often hinges on the length of the visit and the elaborateness of the entertainment. You may take the host and hostess to dinner or to another entertainment, or take the fixings for one evening's meal, which you prepare and serve as a thank-you for their hospitality. Be sure to let your host know ahead of time, however, so he won't make conflicting plans.

Weekend guests from out of town can easily send flowers by making an order over the phone or on the Internet from the comfort of their home and having them delivered to a distant town or city by an associated florist there.

GIFTS FOR ALL OCCASIONS

ANNIVERSARY PARTIES

Older couples celebrating a milestone anniversary often find they have little use for personal gifts and simply want to celebrate their long-term union with friends and loved ones with an anniversary party. It's perfectly correct, in this instance, to include a "No Gifts" written request on the party invitation.

For couples who don't want personal gifts, there is another solution. The persons giving the party can enclose a note with the invitation that says, "In place of gifts, please, if you wish, send a contribution to Mom and Dad's favorite charity." Guests who do so should send a check with a note saying, "Please accept this contribution in honor of the 50th anniversary of Mr. and Mrs. John Doe."

No one giving a twenty-fifth–anniversary party should ever write "No silver" or "No silver gifts, please." That is a clear hint that while the couple does not want silver they do expect other gifts.

It is never proper for a hostess to request a gift of

money for herself. A couple giving their own anniversary party cannot, in good taste, suggest to their friends that they would like gifts of cash.

Unique Gifts for the Anniversary Couple

Enlist the aid of the couple's relatives to gather photos of the couple and their family taken over the course of their marriage. Arrange the photos in a collage-type frame, perhaps leaving a space blank to insert a photo from the anniversary party.

Offer to videotape or photograph the party. When the negatives have been printed, put the photographs in a gift photo album.

Pass around a blank writing album at the party and ask longtime friends and relatives to write a message or anecdote about the couple.

If you do bring a gift, remember that it doesn't have to be composed of the traditional material allotted to each anniversary. But because many people feel that the gift is more meaningful if it is a traditional one, refer to the "Anniversary Materials Suggested Gifts" list, modified in some cases to include modern materials. When an article of the original material cannot be purchased, something similar but not identical may be chosen—for example, a stainless-steel or pewter platter instead of a silver one on a 25th anniversary. For all anniversaries, a lovely flower arrangement or a plant that can be set out in the couple's garden is almost always appropriate.

ANNIVERSARY MATERIALS
SUGGESTED GIFTS LIST

Year	Traditional Anniversary Materials	Suggested Gifts
1	Paper or plastics	Books, notepaper, magazines or newspaper subscriptions
2	Calico or cotton	Cotton napkins and place mats, cotton throw, tapestries
3	Leather or simulated leather	Photo album, leather bag or suitcase
4	Silk or synthetic material	Silk flowers, silk handkerchiefs or scarves
5	Wood	Picture frames, hand-painted wooden trays, wicker baskets
6	Iron	Fireplace tool set, wind chimes
7	Copper or wool	Copper bowls, pots or kettle; wool afghan
8	Electrical appliances	Hand mixer, blender, waffle maker, espresso maker
9	Pottery	Ceramic vase, platter, pitcher, bowl
10	Tin or aluminum	Pretty cookie or biscuit tins, mail-box
11	Steel	Stainless-steel kitchen utensils or bowls
12	Linen	Damask tablecloth
13	Lace	Textiles
14	Formerly ivory now endangered / illegal in most countries	Jewelry
15	Crystal or glass	Christmas ornaments, champagne glasses, carafe

20	China	Hand-painted bowl, platter
25	Silver	Ice bucket, wine bucket
30	Pearls	Pearl-handled steak knives
35	Formerly coral, now endangered	Brooches, figurines
40	Ruby	Jewelry
45	Sapphire	Jewelry
50	Gold	Gold-leaf stationery, jewelry
55	Emerald	Jewelry
60	Diamond	Jewelry
70	Diamond	Jewelry
75	Diamond	Jewelry

BABY SHOWERS

Because babies grow by leaps and bounds, any article of clothing is always a welcome present for new parents. Other useful items: blankets and comforters; even towels and washcloths come in handy.

Personalize a scrapbook with the baby's birth date and all pertinent information, and fill the first few pages with photos of the parents, grandparents, and baby's first home. Include the newspaper and horoscope from the day the baby was born.

It is always thoughtful for a close friend or relative attending a shower to take a big brother or sister a small gift. It is hard enough for young children to learn to share Mommy or Daddy, let alone see piles of presents being given to the interloper!

RELIGIOUS CEREMONIES FOR NEWBORNS

Those invited to a christening or *bris* usually take a gift to the baby since they are presumably close to the family. The gift should be a lasting memento of the occasion and thus is often engraved.

Other typical presents are a silver fork and spoon, a government bond, or a trust fund to which the donor may add each year until the child is grown. Other appropriate gifts are books, toys, and clothing.

RELIGIOUS CONFIRMATION, FIRST COMMUNION, BAR OR BAT MITZVAH

Any of the following are acceptable: prayer book, religious charm or pendant, a gift of money, jewelry, a fine book, or a pen-and-pencil set. Select your gift based on your closeness to the youngster. For other young people, gift certificates for music, clothing, video stores, and fitness centers, as well as sports equipment, are appropriate, depending on the age of the recipient.

SWEET-SIXTEEN AND GRADUATION PARTIES

Birthday gifts for a teenage girl's sweet-sixteen party are generally in the category of gift certificates to a favorite clothes, music, or video store; fashion magazine subscription; personalized stationery; jewelry; perfume; a scarf, belt, or other fashion accessory; cassettes; or CDs.

For teenage boys, clothing, sports equipment, and CDs are generally good choices. Other ideas include video games, computer software, coupons to a local movie theater, or a fitness center gift certificate.

BON VOYAGE PARTIES

Inexpensive is the rule here: small, useful travel-oriented items, such as guidebooks, a trip diary, a travel reading light, a passport folder, money-exchange guide, or a kit of travel-sized toiletries and cleaning products.

If the guests of honor are taking a cruise, arrange with the wine steward to have champagne or wine served as a surprise during the voyage.

Give extra rolls of film and include a prepaid processing mailer that allows travelers to be greeted by their photos when they return home.

Every traveler to a foreign country needs a certain amount of small-denomination bills and loose change for tips and cab fare when they first arrive at their destination. Give the traveler the equivalent of 20 dollars' worth of bills and change in the currency of the country he or she is visiting.

GLOBAL GIFT-GIVING

The giving of gifts internationally varies from country to country. You would be wise to find out ahead of time what kinds of gifts are appropriate—and *when* it is appropriate to give them. Consider the following:

• Make sure you aren't committing a terrible breach of etiquette by presenting a gift that is offensive to your host. You would never give a gift of cowhide in India, for example, where the cow is considered sacred, just as you would not present a gift of flowers in Japan, as flowers there are given only in the event of courtship, illness, or death.

• Timing is important. In Middle Eastern countries and in Japan, you should not be the first to present a gift, as this causes your host to lose face. Wait instead for the host to give you a gift or token, and be prepared to reciprocate immediately and in kind. In Russia, gifts are often given at a dinner during toasts, but rarely in an office or conference room.

• When visiting the home of your host in another country, you should bring gifts for any children in the house.

• In certain countries, a bottle of wine or liquor is not an appropriate gift.

• Certain flowers often have symbolic meaning in other countries; before selecting a bouquet for your host, find out whether the flowers you choose are appropriate. White flowers, for example, are symbols of mourning in the Far East, as are gladiolus and chrysanthemums in many other countries. Yellow flowers have negative connotations in Peru, Mexico, and Iran, where they are associated with hate or mourning.

10 GREAT HOUSEWARMING GIFTS

1. Take a photograph of your friends in front of their new home. Have a print made, then frame and wrap it.

2. Create a keepsake with an attractive guest book. Place it at the door of the new house and have all the guests sign it, adding comments, addresses, and phone numbers. Present it to the hosts at the end of the party.

3. Put together, with several other neighbors, if you wish, an old-fashioned welcome wagon–style basket of staples a homeowner can't do without. A beribboned basket full of nails, notepads, a screwdriver, tape, a corkscrew—even a toilet plunger—makes a fun and useful offering.

4. Have each of your neighbors prepare a casserole that can be frozen to give to the new neighbor to thaw and cook when busy with unpacking and renovating.

5. Give personalized return address labels of the new address.

6. Put together jars of fresh spices by visiting a store that sells freshly ground spices in bulk and buying four to six empty glass jars. Fill the jars and place handwritten labels on each.

7. Present an address book listing the names, addresses, and phone numbers of recommended local services and stores.

8. Give a subscription to the local newspaper of the new town or area.

9. Prepare a basket full of garden bulbs and seeds.

10. Present discount coupons to local movie theaters, restaurants, and shops.

CHAPTER 17

MEALTIME MANNERS

Consideration for others is what translates into good table manners. Whether you're seated across the dinner table from a U.S. senator or your host's fifteen-year-old son, show that person respect by demonstrating good table manners. Here is a guide to some of the most common situations you'll face at the dinner table.

MANNERS AT THE TABLE

THE CORRECT WAY TO USE A KNIFE AND FORK.
The American custom of "zigzag" eating (changing the fork from the left to the right hand after cutting) is perfectly correct. The knife is put down on the plate after cutting and the fork is raised to the mouth, tines up. Equally correct is the European method of leaving the fork in the left hand after cutting and raising it to the mouth in the same position in which it was held for cutting, tines down. The knife may also be used as a "pusher" if necessary. To do so, hold the knife in the left hand in the same position as when cutting with the right hand, and the tip of the blade helps to guide and push the food onto the fork.

CORRECT SILVER PLACEMENT. When the main course is finished, the knife and fork are placed beside each other on the dinner plate diagonally from upper left to lower right, the handles extended slightly over the edge of the plate. The dessert spoon and/or fork is placed in the same position on the plate when the diner has finished. If dessert is served in a stemmed or deep bowl on another plate, the dessert spoon is put down on the plate, never left in the bowl.

ELBOWS ON OR OFF THE TABLE? In some situations elbows are not only permitted on the table but actually necessary. This is true in certain places, such as noisy restaurants, where the only way to hear above the chatter and dishes is to lean far forward. One is far more graceful leaning forward supported by his or her elbows than doubled forward over hands in the lap. At a formal dinner, elbows may be on the table if one has to lean forward in order to talk to a companion at a distance across the table. But even in these special situations elbows are *never* on the table *when one is eating*.

WHICH SILVER TO USE—AND WHEN. *You always start with the implement of each type that is farthest from the plate.* Of course, if the table is incorrectly set, and you realize that you cannot use the implement for the course that its position indicates, it makes sense to choose the next one that is appropriate. Otherwise, start at the outside, working your way with each course toward the center.

How to hold flatware. Lightly. The fork and spoon are held with the thumb and forefinger at a position on the fork that is comfortable, usually about three-quarters of the way up the handle. Your other three fingers then fit loosely and comfortably behind the handle, with the middle finger serving as a support from underneath.

Reaching across the table. Stretching to retrieve a serving dish, say, is only correct when it does not involve stretching across your neighbor or leaning far across the table yourself. If the item you want is not close at hand, simply ask the person closest to it to pass it to you.

Pass the salt, pass the pepper? There is no rule that says you have to pass both at once. Sometimes it simply makes sense to do so.

How to hold a serving spoon and fork. When lifting food from a serving dish, the spoon is held underneath, with the fork prongs turned down to help hold the portion on the spoon.

Second helpings? The circumstances determine whether or not it is acceptable to ask for seconds at a dinner party. It is not acceptable at a formal dinner but is permissible at an informal one. At a formal dinner second helpings are to be offered.

How to break bread. Help yourself to bread using your fingers. Place the bread, roll, crackers, or whatever on your butter plate. Don't butter the whole piece at once, but instead break off manageable pieces, and butter and eat them one at a time.

BIG DOS AND DON'TS OF GRACIOUS DINING

A review of the following will help make any host or guest at any table comfortable, relaxed, and proficient at gracious dining.

- Do remember to say "please" and "thank you" frequently.
- Do eat quietly. Do not slurp, smack your lips, crunch, or make other noises as you chew or swallow.
- Do always chew with your mouth closed.
- Do chew your food well, putting your utensils down between bites.
- Do wipe your fingers and your mouth frequently with your napkin. Use a corner of the napkin and blot at your mouth; don't wad up the napkin and scrub your face with it.
- Don't encircle your plate with your arm.
- Don't push your plate back when finished, or lean back and announce, "I'm through" or "I'm stuffed." Putting your utensils down across your plate will suffice to show you have finished.
- Don't put liquids in your mouth if it is already

filled with food—and don't take huge mouthfuls of anything at any time.

- Don't crook your finger when picking up a cup or glass. It's an affected mannerism.
- Don't leave your spoon in your cup, soup bowl, or stemmed glass.
- Don't cut up your entire meal before you start to eat. Cut only one or two bites at a time.
- Don't leave half the food on your spoon or fork. Learn to put less on and then eat it in one bite.
- Don't wear an excessive amount of lipstick to the table. Not only can it stain napkins, but it also looks unattractive on the rims of cups and glasses or on the silver. It's a good idea to blot your lipstick prior to dining.

NAPKIN NO-NOS

Do not open your napkin with a violent shake. Unfold it as much as necessary with both hands.

Never tuck a napkin into a collar, belt, or between the buttons of your shirt.

When using the napkin, avoid wiping your mouth as if with a washcloth. Blotting or patting the lips is much more appropriate.

When the meal is finished, or if you leave the table during the meal, do not refold or crumple up your napkin. Put the napkin on the left side of your place or, if the plates have been removed, in the center. It should be laid on the table in loose folds so that it does not spread itself out. Another option when leaving the table during a meal is to leave your napkin on your chair, so others needn't see it. At a dinner party the hostess lays her napkin on the table as a signal that the meal is over, and the guests then lay their napkins on the table—not before.

Do not reinsert napkins into napkin rings at the end of a dinner.

WHEN I'M A GUEST AT A DINNER PARTY, WHAT DO I DO WHEN I . . .

Q. . . . need to cough, sneeze, or blow my nose?

A. You should excuse yourself from the table and go to the restroom to blow your nose. You might find it necessary to first blow your nose (by way of a few gentle puffs), using your handkerchief or tissue immediately following a sneeze. Do not use your napkin to blow your nose. Before returning to the table, be sure to wash your hands thoroughly after you're through.

Q. . . . discover bugs, hair, or other nonedibles in the food?

A. Try to remove the object without calling attention to it and continue eating. If you are truly repulsed, leave the dish untouched rather than embarrass your hostess in a private home. At a restaurant you may— and should—quietly point out the critter to your waiter and ask for a replacement dish. If the alien object has reached your mouth without your previously noticing it, remove it with your fingers as inconspicuously as possible and place it at the edge of your plate.

Q. . . . get food stuck in a tooth?

A. It is not permissible to use a toothpick or to use your fingers to pick at your teeth when at the table. If something stuck in your tooth is actually hurting, excuse yourself from the table and go to the restroom to remove it. Otherwise, wait until the end of the meal and then go take care of it, asking for a toothpick if necessary.

Q. . . . spill something?

A. Pick up jelly, a bit of vegetable, or other solid food with the blade of your knife or a clean spoon. If the spill has caused a stain, and you are a guest at someone's house, dab a little water from your glass on it with the corner of your napkin. Apologize to your hostess, who, in turn, should not add to your embarrassment by calling attention to the accident. At an informal dinner without help, offer to get a cloth or sponge to mop up the liquid and help the hostess clean up in any way you can.

Q. . . . begin choking on meat or bones?

A. If a sip of water does not help but a good cough will, cover your mouth with your napkin and cough. Remove the morsel with your fingers and put it on the edge of your plate. If you continue to cough, excuse yourself from the table. In the event that you are really choking, you will be unable to speak. Don't hesitate to get someone's attention to help you. The seriousness of your condition will quickly be recognized, and it is no time to worry about manners. Keeping calm and acting quickly might well save your life.

Q. . . . am faced with a finger bowl?

A. Finger bowls are generally small glass bowls filled halfway to three-quarters of the way with cold water and are most often seen at formal meals. They are there for the purpose of freshening one's fingers after a meal or after eating a hands-on food such as snails, corn on the cob, or hard-shelled seafood. Finger bowls are placed at the side of each diner's place after a hands-on dinner, or on the dessert plate at a formal dinner.

Dip your fingers, one hand at a time, into the water and then dry your fingers on your napkin. If a finger bowl is brought directly before dessert, it is often placed on a doily on the dessert plate. To remove it, lift it, with the doily underneath, and move it to the upper left of your place setting.

A slice of lemon is never used in a finger bowl at a formal dinner, but flowers may be floated in it. Lemon may be floated in a finger bowl used after a lobster dinner.

In some restaurants, moist steamed hand towels are brought to the table at the conclusion of the meal. These are held in tongs and presented to the diner. Take the towel, use it to wipe your hands and, if necessary, around your mouth. Diligent waiters will hover and take the towel from you the minute you are finished. If your waiter disappears, just put the towel at the side of your place on the table.

Q. . . . have to use a saltcellar?

A. Some hostesses prefer to use old-fashioned saltcellars, which salt shakers have largely replaced. If there is no spoon in the saltcellar, use the tip of a clean knife to take some salt. If the saltcellar is for you alone, you may either use the tip of your knife or you may take a pinch with your fingers. If it is to be shared with others, never use your fingers or a knife that is not clean. Salt that is to be dipped into should be put on the bread-and-butter plate or on the rim of whatever plate is before you.

Q. . . . eat food that is too hot or food that tastes spoiled?

A. If a bite of food is too hot, quickly take a swallow of water. If there is no cold beverage at all, and your mouth is scalding, you can spit the food out, preferably onto your fork or into your fingers, and from there place it quickly on the edge of the plate. The same is true of spoiled food. Should you eat a bad oyster or clam, for example, don't swallow it. Remove it as quickly and unobtrusively as you can. To spit anything whatsoever into the corner of your napkin is not permissible.

COCKTAIL AND HORS D'OEUVRES SAVVY

When you are served a beverage with a spoon or swizzle stick (stirrer) in it, remove it from the glass before drinking. Do not drink with anything, whether a paper umbrella or a teaspoon, still in the cup or glass in which it is served. At someone's home, you would put a spoon on the saucer, on a plate, or on a paper napkin, never on the tablecloth or on a cloth napkin.

If the appetizer you put in your mouth does not agree with your taste buds, you may gently push it with your tongue into a cocktail napkin held in your hand, which you will then dispose of in an appropriate waste receptacle.

If toothpicks are offered, spear the hors d'oeuvre, put it in your mouth, and then place the used toothpick on a plate or receptacle put out for that purpose, or hold it in your napkin until you can find a waste basket. Never put a used toothpick back on the serving tray. Do not discard toothpicks, napkins, uneaten appetizers, or remnants in ashtrays, a potentially hazardous practice should a lighted cigarette be placed there.

When fresh vegetables and dip are offered, only dip the vegetable once, never a second time, after taking a bite of the vegetable. If fresh vegetables are passed as a relish at the table, place them on your bread-and-butter plate or, if there isn't one, on your salad plate or on the edge of whatever plate is in front of you. Never transfer a relish or olive directly from the serving plate to your mouth.

If you want to eat the olives, cherries, or onions served in cocktails, by all means do so. If they are served on a toothpick or cocktail pick, simply remove them from the drink and enjoy them. If there is no pick, drink enough of the cocktail so that you will not wet your fingers, and lift out the olive or cherry and eat it with your fingers.

RESTAURANT TABLE MANNERS

Do restaurant table manners differ from the manners one uses at home? Although table manners are much the same whether you are eating at home or at a restaurant, a few special situations arise when dining out.

When vegetables and potatoes are served in individual side dishes, you may eat them directly from small dishes or put them on your dinner plate by using a serving spoon or sliding them directly out of the small dish. Ask the waiter to remove any empty dishes, to avoid an overcrowded table.

When an uncut loaf of bread is placed on the

table, the host—or the diner closest to the bread—slices or breaks off two or three individual portions and offers them with the rest of the loaf in the bread-basket or on the plate to the people beside him. This is then passed around the table for diners to cut the bread for themselves and possibly their neighbors.

If coffee or tea is placed on the table without first having been poured by the waiter, the person nearest the pot should offer to pour, filling his or her own cup last.

If sugar, crackers, cream, or other accompaniments to meals are served with paper wrappers or in plastic or cardboard containers, the wrappers should be crumpled up tightly and either tucked under the rim of your plate or placed on the edge of the saucer or butter plate. Don't put them in the ashtray if smokers are present, since their lighted cigarettes could easily set the paper on fire.

Don't wipe off tableware in a restaurant. If your silverware is dirty, simply ask the waiter or waitress for a clean one. If you spill wine or water in a restaurant, try to quietly attract the attention of the waiter.

When you are dining at a restaurant buffet, never go back to the buffet for a refill with a dirty plate. Leave it for the waitperson to pick up and start afresh with a clean plate.

Tasting another person's food at the table is permissible if done unobtrusively. Never reach over and spear something off someone else's plate, however, or feed someone across the table. Either hand your fork to your dinner partner, have them spear a bite and then hand it back to you, or have them place a portion on your plate.

At the end of a meal a woman may quickly put on a little lipstick, but to look in a mirror and daub at the face is in bad taste.

The one never-to-be-broken rule is: Never use a comb at a restaurant table—or in any public place. Never rearrange or put your hands to your hair in any place where food is served. These rules apply to both men and women.

TABLE MANNERS FOR CHILDREN

BE NEAT AND CLEAN. Make hand-washing a habit. Teach your child to wash his hands and face before he comes to a table to eat. Instead of ordering children to do this, tell them why. Explain about germs and how pleasant it is to eat and talk with someone who made herself look nice, out of respect for everyone else. When children understand the reason for doing something, it is easier for them to remember to do it.

EAT IN SMALL BITES. First, because it isn't safe to have more in your mouth than you can manage, and second, because it is unattractive to sit with anyone who can't close his lips or who has bits of food spewing from his mouth. Thus, chew with the mouth closed.

DO NOT FLOAT FOOD DOWN YOUR THROAT WITH DRINKS. Again, there is a safety factor at work, but there is also a politeness factor, since a child has to open a mouthful of food in order to swallow a beverage. A rule could be that the mouth opens to receive a spoonful or forkful of food, and it doesn't open again until that food is chewed, with the mouth closed, and swallowed.

FOOD NOISES ARE UNACCEPTABLE. Lips are not smacked; drinks are not gulped.

NAPKINS, NOT SLEEVES OR HANDS, ARE FOR WIPING MOUTHS. They are meant to be used regularly throughout the meal. Why? Because it is hard for anyone to know if he has a milk mustache or ketchup on his cheek. Using the napkin periodically takes care of what otherwise might be an embarrassing sight.

THERE IS A CORRECT WAY TO HOLD AND USE UTENSILS. Start out with younger children using a spoon. By age five or six most children can learn to be adept at using a fork and knife. By age six, children should learn how to cut food and how to properly hold a fork and spoon: not in a fist, but comfortably with the thumb and forefinger, about three-quarters of the way down the handle.

LEARN TO MAKE PLEASANT MEALTIME CONVERSATION. Do not criticize the food, and do thank the hostess or cook upon finishing the meal.

ASK IF YOU WISH TO BE EXCUSED FROM THE TABLE. Children should be permitted to be excused from the table, when very young, if the meal is an extended one. Expecting a young child to sit quietly through a protracted meal when his food is gone is an unreasonable demand on his patience and ability to sit still without wiggling, fiddling, and noisemaking to help pass the time. "May I please be excused?" should be asked of parents or of the hostess when dining with friends and relatives.

HOW TO EAT CERTAIN FOODS

The basic etiquette of eating all foods is that they be transported to the mouth in manageable, bite-sized pieces. Certain courses and foods, however, require special dexterity. One of the greatest tests a gracious diner faces is to be presented with a food he is unfamiliar with. Yet even familiar foods can be challenging when dining in a formal setting, where some dishes aren't meant to be eaten as casually as you might eat them at home.

When presented with a food you have never eaten before, such as escargots, what you do depends on the company you are in. If among friends, there is nothing embarrassing about saying, "I've never had escargots before. Please show me how to do this." If you're at a formal function or among strangers, however, you may not want to admit to this. In this case, it is best to delay beginning by having a sip of water or wine and watching what others are doing.

Certain foods, such as chicken drumsticks, are generally eaten in informal settings with the fingers, and in many homes, asparagus is a finger food. But what happens when a diner at a formal table is faced with asparagus drenched in Hollandaise sauce? Does he pluck a spear with his fingers, throw his head back, and toss the sauce-laden vegetable into his mouth, dripping Hollandaise down his pleated shirt? Or does he follow the lead of other diners and cut his spears neatly with knife and fork? (The correct answer: the latter.) The primary advice on how to eat particular foods, then, is to take into consideration the properties of the foods, how they are served, and to gauge the environment before proceeding.

APPLES AND PEARS

Slice into quarters, core each quarter, and cut into slices, which are then eaten with the fingers.

APRICOTS

See Cherries, Apricots, and Plums.

ARTICHOKES

Whole artichokes are always eaten with the fingers. Begin at the outside base of the artichoke and pull off one leaf at a time. Dip the base of the leaf, which is the softer meaty end of it, into melted butter, if provided, and then place it between your teeth and pull it forward. The leaves closer to the center will have a greater edible portion than those at the outside. Place the inedible portion of each leaf neatly on the side of your plate.

When the leaves are all consumed and you reach the center of the artichoke, scrape away the thistle-like part with your knife. This fuzzy portion is inedible and is called the choke. Place this along the side of your plate with the leaves. The remaining part of the artichoke is the heart, or bottom. Cut this into bite-size pieces with a knife and fork and dip the pieces into the melted butter before eating.

Asparagus

Although asparagus is by reputation a finger food, you should always use utensils to eat it at all but the most informal dining situations. When it is prepared al dente so that the stalks are firm, and any sauce is only on the tips, you may pick it up with your fingers, one stalk at a time, and eat it from the tip to the opposite end in manageable bites. When the stalks are covered in sauce or are limp, then cut them with your fork or fork and knife and eat them in small pieces. All hard ends should be cut off asparagus before it is served. If this has not been done, do not attempt to eat the ends: If you can't cut them, you can't chew them.

AVOCADOS

When avocado slices are served, cut and eat with a fork. When avocados are served in halves, hold the shell to steady it with one hand and eat the fruit with a spoon. Leave the empty shell, which is inedible, on the plate. When a salad or other mixture is served in an avocado shell, it is permissible to hold the shell lightly with one hand while eating the contents with a fork held in the other hand.

BACON

Eat breakfast bacon with a fork if limp; if it is dry and crisp, you may use your fingers in informal settings.

BANANAS

Peel halfway down and eat bite by bite at the family table, but when dining out it is better to peel the skin all the way off, lay the fruit on your plate, cut it in slices, and eat it with a fork.

BEVERAGES, HOT

When served in a cup with a saucer, place the spoon at the side of the saucer, as you do a tea bag. If the beverage slops onto a saucer, and no replacement is available, it is fine to pour the liquid back into the cup and use a paper napkin to dry the bottom of the cup. When your hot beverage is served in a mug, never leave the spoon in the mug. If the tablecloth or mats are fabric, rest the bowl of the spoon facedown on the edge of a butter or dinner plate, with the handle on the table. If the tablecloth is paper or plastic, you may lick the spoon clean and lay it beside the mug. Beverages that are too hot to drink may be sipped, never slurped, from a spoon.

BREAD AND BUTTER

Break the bread with your fingers into moderate-sized pieces. To butter it, hold a piece on the edge of the bread-and-butter plate and spread enough butter on it for a mouthful or two at a time. If there is no butter knife, use any other knife that is available.

BREAD, ROUND LOAF ON CUTTING BOARD

Some restaurants present an entire round loaf of bread on a cutting board for you to slice yourself. This should be cut not like a round cake in wedges, but in slices. Starting at one side, thinly slice the crust off, and then slice toward the center.

BREAKFAST PASTRIES

Cut Danish pastry or sticky buns in half or in quarters with a knife and eat with the fingers, if not too sticky, or with a fork. Cut muffins in half either vertically or horizontally, and butter one half at a time. Open and butter croissants or popovers, and then eat in small pieces.

BUTTER

Butter bread, biscuits, toast, pancakes, and corn on the cob with a knife. For corn that has been cut off the cob, rice, or potatoes, mix butter in it with a fork.

When pats of butter are served, lift them with the utensil provided (most often a butter knife or small fork) and transfer them to your own plate. When butter is served as a block, cut a pat from one end and transfer to your bread-and-butter plate or dinner plate. If there is no accompanying utensil, transfer the butter with your own clean knife. When butter is presented in a tub, scoop a portion with your own knife or butter knife and place it on your bread-and-butter plate or dinner plate.

In a restaurant, when butter is offered in individually wrapped squares, open the wrapper and use your knife to push the square onto your plate, folding the buttery side of the wrapper in and placing it on the edge of the plate, never on the tablecloth.

CANTALOUPES AND MELONS

Served in halves or wedges, melons should be eaten with a spoon. When served in precut pieces, eat with a fork.

CAVIAR

Use the spoon with which it is presented to place the caviar on your plate. Using your own knife or spoon, then place small amounts on toast triangles, which may be buttered or not. If chopped egg, minced onions, or sour cream are served with caviar, one or more of these toppings is spooned, sparingly, on top of the caviar.

CHERRIES, APRICOTS, AND PLUMS

Eat with the fingers. The pit of the fruit should be made as clean as possible in your mouth and then dropped into your almost closed, cupped hand, and then to your plate. Plums and apricots are held in your fingers and eaten as close to the pit as possible. When you remove a pit with your fingers, do so with your thumb underneath and your first two fingers across your mouth, not with your fingertips pointing into your mouth. Or push the pit forward with the tongue onto a spoon and then drop it onto a plate.

CHERRY TOMATOES

Except when served in a salad or other dish, cherry tomatoes are eaten with the fingers. And they *squirt*! The best thing to do is to try to select one small enough to be put in your mouth whole. Even then, close your lips tightly before chewing. If you must bite into a larger one, make a little break in the skin with your front teeth before biting it in half. When served whole in a salad or other dish, cherry tomatoes are cut, carefully, with a knife and fork and eaten with the fork.

CHICKEN, TURKEY, AND OTHER FOWL

At a formal dinner, no part of a bird is picked up with the fingers. However, among family and friends and in family-style or informal restaurants, it is permissible to do so—particularly if it is fried.

The main body of the bird, however, is not eaten with the fingers. Cut off as much meat as you can from the main body and leave the rest on your plate. To eat the small bones, such as the joint or wing, hold the piece of bone with meat on it up to your mouth and eat it clean. Larger joints, too, such as the drumstick of a roast chicken, may be picked up after the first few easily cut pieces have been eaten.

CHOPS

At a dinner party or in a formal restaurant, lamb chops must be eaten with knife and fork. Cut the center, or eye, of the chop off the bone into two or three pieces. At the family table or in an informal group of friends, the center may be cut out and eaten with the fork, and the bone picked up and eaten clean with the teeth. This is permissible, too, with veal or pork chops, but only when they are broiled or otherwise served without sauce. When picking up a chop with your fingers, hold it with one hand only. If it is too big to hold with only one hand, it is too big to pick up.

CLAMS, MUSSELS, AND OYSTERS

Clams and oysters on the half shell are generally served on cracked ice and arranged around a container of cocktail sauce. Hold the shell with the fingers of your left hand and the shellfish fork (or smallest fork provided) with the right hand. Spear the clam or oyster with the fork, dip it into sauce, and eat it in one bite. If a part of the clam or oyster sticks to the shell, use your fork to separate it from the shell. Or take a little of the sauce on your fork and drop it onto the clam or squeeze a little lemon onto it before eating it.

When raw clams or oysters are ordered at a clam bar or eaten at a picnic, you may pick up the shell with the fingers and suck the clam or oyster and its juice right off the shell.

Steamed clams should be open at least halfway. If they aren't, don't eat them; it means they were dead before they were cooked, and therefore could cause illness if eaten. Open the shell fully, holding it with your left hand, and pull out the clam with your fingers if the setting is informal, or with a seafood fork if it is more formal. If the clam is a true steamer, slip the skin off the neck with your fingers and put it aside. Holding it by the neck, dip the steamed clam into broth and/or melted butter and eat in one bite. Empty shells are placed in a bowl provided for that purpose, or around the edge of your plate if there is no bowl.

Mussels, like some steamed clams, may be served in their shells in the broth in which they are steamed. The mussel may be removed from its shell with a fork, then dipped into the sauce and eaten in one bite. It is permissible to pick up the shell, scooping a little of the juice with it, and suck the mussel and juice directly off the shell. The juice or broth remaining in the bowl may be eaten with a spoon, or you may sop it up with pieces of a roll or French bread speared on the tines of your fork.

CORN ON THE COB

Eat it as neatly and gently as possible. If melted butter has not been added in the kitchen, take pats of butter from the butter plate and place them on your dinner plate. Butter and season only a few rows of the corn at a time, repeating this process until the corn is finished.

FETTUCCINE

See Spaghetti, Linguini, and Fettuccine.

FISH

Fish served in fillet form is eaten with a fork and knife. If you find small bones in your mouth when eating fish, push them to the front of your mouth with your tongue and then onto your fork, removing them to the side of the plate.

FOWL

See Chicken, Turkey, and Other Fowl.

FRENCH FRIES

When French-fried potatoes accompany finger foods, such as hamburgers, hot dogs, or other sandwiches, they may be eaten with the fingers—unless they are covered with sauce, such as ketchup. At other times they should be cut into reasonable lengths and eaten with a fork.

GRAPES

Avoid pulling grapes off the bunch one at a time. Instead, choose a branch with several grapes on it and break it off or cut off with scissors. Seedless grapes are no problem to eat at all, since the entire fruit, skin and all, is eaten. Grapes with seeds, however, are more of a challenge and can be eaten one of two ways. First, you may lay the grape on its side, holding it with the fingers of one hand, and cut in the center with the point of a knife, which also lifts and removes the seeds. Or pop the grape in your mouth whole and then deposit the seeds into your fingers and place them on your plate as elegantly as possible. Concord or garden grapes with difficult-to-digest skin should be pressed between your lips and against your almost-closed teeth so that the juice and pulp will be drawn into your mouth and the skin left to be discarded.

GRAVIES AND SAUCES

You may sop bread into gravy, but it must be done by putting a small piece down on the gravy and then eating it with your fork as though it were any other helping on your plate. If it's easier for you, you may put it into your mouth "continental" style, with the tines pointed down as they were when you sopped up the gravy. A good sauce may also be finished in this way.

ICED TEA OR COFFEE

If it is served on a saucer, rest the spoon on that. If not, rest the spoon as you would a spoon served with a mug, as described in the section Beverages, Hot.

KIWI

Peel this fuzzy-skinned fruit and slice like a tomato. If presented with an unpeeled kiwi, use a sharp paring knife to peel away the outer skin, which is inedible, and slice the kiwi crosswise, further cutting it into bite-size pieces and eating it with a fork. The seeds are edible.

LASAGNA

See Ziti, Lasagna, and Layered Pasta.

LINGUINI

See Spaghetti, Linguini, and Fettuccine.

LOBSTER

It's a good idea to crack lobster shells at all points before you serve them. Provide each guest with individual nutcrackers or shellfish crackers to finish the process—as well as with seafood forks for extracting the lobster meat. Place a large bowl or platter for discarded empty shells on the table and give a big paper napkin or plastic bib to each lobster eater.

Crack claws slowly so that the juice does not squirt when the shell breaks. Holding the lobster steady with one hand and the nutcracker in your other hand, twist off the claws from the body and place them on the side of your plate. Crack each claw and pull out the meat. The meat is removed from the large claw ends and from each joint with a shellfish fork or a knife. The tail meat is pulled out of the shell in two solid pieces—one side at a time. Cut into bite-sized pieces and dip into melted butter, if hot, or mayonnaise, if cold. The red roe and the green "fat" or "tamale" are edible and delectable to some, who like to combine it with the lobster meat. Real lobster lovers get an additional morsel out of the legs by breaking off one at a time, putting them into the mouth and biting up the shell, squeezing the meat out of the broken end.

The host should have finger bowls with warm water and lemon slices at the side of each place as soon as people are finished eating. These are carried away after the dinner plates have been removed.

MEATS, BARBECUED

Because the nature of a barbecue is informal, eating barbecued foods should be informal. When ribs, chicken pieces, hamburgers, and hot dogs are served, use your fingers. Eat steak, fish, and other meats served in larger portions with a fork.

MELONS

See Cantaloupes and Melons.

MUSSELS

See Clams, Mussels, and Oysters.

OLIVES

Eat olives with your fingers when they are served as a relish. If there are stones, bite off the meat of the olive, but don't actually "clean" the stone. Remove the stone from your mouth with your fingers, or by pushing it with your tongue onto a spoon. Bite a large stuffed olive in half. Put only a very small one in your mouth whole. When the olive is in a salad, eat it with your fork, not your fingers.

ORANGES AND TANGERINES

Eat these citrus fruits by slicing the two ends of the rind off first and then cutting the peel off in vertical strips. If the peel is thick and loose, it can be pulled off with the fingers. Tangerines are easily broken apart into small sections by hand, while oranges may need to be cut with a knife. Seeds should be taken out from the center with the tip of the knife and sections eaten with the fingers. If there is fiber around the peeled orange or tangerine, it may be removed with the fingers. Any remaining fiber and seeds can be removed from the mouth neatly with the thumb and first two fingers (fingers above and thumb underneath).

OYSTERS

See Clams, Mussels, and Oysters.

PASTA, LAYERED

See Ziti, Lasagna, and Layered Pasta.

PASTRIES

See Breakfast Pastries.

PEAS

Peas are perhaps one of the most difficult foods to capture and eat. You may use your knife as a pusher to get them onto your fork, or you may use the tines of the fork to actually spear a few peas at a time.

PEACHES

Peel and then eat with knife and fork.

PEARS

See Apples and Pears.

PIE

Eat with a fork; if à la mode, you may use a spoon.

PINEAPPLE

This prickly tropical fruit is sliced into round

pieces and served on a plate to be eaten with a dessert fork or spoon.

PIZZA

Pizza is cut into wedges with a knife or pizza cutter and served this way. Individual wedges may be picked up and eaten with the fingers. Some pizza lovers prefer to fold the pizza vertically at the center to keep edges from hanging outward and dripping before lifting it to their mouths. Pizza may also be cut into bite-size pieces with a knife and fork and eaten with a fork.

PLUMS

See Cherries, Apricots, and Plums.

SALAD

If your salad has large leaves of lettuce, it is perfectly acceptable to cut the lettuce with a knife and fork into small pieces. Cut only one or two bites at a time. Never attack your entire salad, cutting the entire plateful into small pieces at once.

SANDWICHES

All ordinary sandwiches are eaten with the fingers. Club sandwiches and other sandwiches an inch or more thick are best cut into small portions before being picked up and held tightly in the fingers of both hands. Naturally, sandwiches that are served with gravy, such as hot turkey or roast beef sandwiches, are cut with a knife and fork and eaten with a fork.

SASHIMI

See Sushi and Sashimi.

SAUCES

See Gravies and Sauces.

SHISH KEBAB

Except for small shish kebab served as an hors d'oeuvre, you do not eat directly from the skewer. When shish kebab is served as a main course, lift the skewer with one hand, and with the other, use your fork, beginning with the pieces at the bottom, to push and slide the meat and vegetables off the skewer and onto your plate. Place the emptied skewer on the edge of your plate, and with your knife and fork, cut the meat and vegetables into manageable pieces a bite at a time.

SHRIMP COCKTAIL

If not too large, each shrimp should be eaten in one bite. When shrimp are of jumbo size, the diner has no alternative but to grasp the cup in which they are served firmly with one hand and cut the shrimp as neatly as possible with the edge of the fork. It is impractical to use a knife because the stemmed shrimp cup will tip over unless held with one hand. If the saucer or plate under the shrimp cup is large enough, you might remove a shrimp from the cup, place it on the saucer, and cut it there with a knife and fork. The problem can be avoided by arranging shrimp attractively on a small plate—where they can easily be cut with knife or fork. When shrimp are served as an hors d'oeuvre, pick them up by their tails, dip them (once) into the sauce, and then discard the tail into the receptacle provided.

Eat shrimp cocktail with the smallest fork at your place. If a lemon wedge is served with the shrimp, spear it with your fork and, covering the back of the wedge with your other hand, squeeze it carefully over the shrimp. If individual sauce bowls are offered, dip your shrimp into the sauce. If the sauce dish is shared, spoon it from the dish over the shrimp.

SNAILS (ESCARGOTS)

Grasp snail shells with a special holder or with the fingers of one hand if no holder is provided. With the other hand, remove the meat with a small fork.

Pour any garlic butter that remains in the shells onto the snail plate and sop up with small pieces of French bread on the end of a fork.

SOUP

If the soup is served in a cup with handles, you may pick up the cup or just use a spoon. When served in a shallow soup plate and the level of soup is so low that you must tip the plate to avoid scraping the bottom, lift the near edge and tip the plate away from you, never toward you. Spoon the soup either away from you or toward you, whichever is less awkward. Soups such as French onion, which is served with a crouton in the bowl and cheese baked and bubbled on the top, require two utensils for eating. The soup spoon is used to eat the soup, while a knife or even a fork is required to cut the cheese on the rim of the soup cup or dish so that it does not trail from bowl to mouth in a long string. Initially, when the bowl is full and there is danger of splashing, it is not incorrect to take a small amount of the cheese on the spoon and twist it around the bowl of the spoon, cutting it neatly at the edge with the fork or knife. The spoon may then be dipped into the bowl so a spoonful of soup is eaten with the cheese already on the spoon.

SPAGHETTI, LINGUINI, AND FETTUCCINE

There are three ways to eat stringy pasta—none difficult to master. The first is to take a few strands on your fork and twirl the spaghetti around the fork, holding the tines against the edge of your plate. The second is to hold the fork in one hand and a large, dessert-size spoon in the other. Take a few strands of the pasta on the fork and place the tines against the bowl of the spoon, twirling the fork to wrap the spaghetti around itself as it turns. The third is simply to cut spaghetti (linguini, fettuccine, or other long pasta) into sections and eat it with a fork.

If the first two methods are used, the spaghetti should be twirled until there are no dangling ends. Bring the fork to your mouth. If ends do unwind themselves from around the fork, you must either suck them (quietly, please!) into your mouth, or bite them neatly, hoping they fall back onto your fork and do not drop to your chest or plate.

When pasta is served with the sauce ladled on top and not mixed in, mix it neatly, using a fork and spoon, before eating.

SUSHI AND SASHIMI

Sushi is served in small pieces that may be eaten whole, either with the fingers or chopsticks. Bites may be taken of sushi that is soft—certain sushi fish is difficult to bite in half, such as *tako* (octopus), and so should be popped into the mouth whole if possible. If eaten with chopsticks, the sushi is picked up and eaten from the chopsticks whole or in bites. Soy sauce is provided for dipping if one wishes: a small amount (to taste) of *wasabi* (green Japanese horseradish paste) is taken on the chopsticks and mixed gently into the soy sauce in an individual dish provided for this. Then one end of the sushi portions may be dipped into it and put in the mouth. The sliced pickled ginger that is provided can be eaten as a palate cleanser. Sashimi, which is thinly sliced boneless fish, is eaten with chopsticks and not with fingers, dipping in the manner explained above. If you are serving yourself from a serving platter of sushi or sashimi, check to see if the server has provided a set of serving chopsticks (which are a bit bigger than dining chopsticks). If they have not been provided, you may serve yourself from the tray, taking a few pieces of sushi or sashimi at a time onto your small tray/plate provided, then taking more as needed. If you have been served rice separately with another Japanese or Asian dish, also be certain not to leave chopsticks sticking up from a bowl of rice.

TACOS AND TORTILLAS

Eat tacos and tortillas with the hands—it is impossible to cut into the crisp shell with a knife and fork without having it crack and crumble. Eat any filling that falls out, however with a fork, not with your hands.

TANGERINES

See Oranges and Tangerines.

TORTILLAS

See Tacos and Tortillas.

TURKEY

See Chicken, Turkey, and Other Fowl.

ZITI, LASAGNA, AND LAYERED PASTA

Melted, stringy mozzarella cheese from layered pasta dishes can stubbornly stretch from the dish to your mouth and be difficult to cut off. Before you take a bite, slice portions and cut through the cheese. This prevents the rather unattractive sight of strings of cheese hanging from your mouth and chin as you dine.

CHAPTER 18

ACCIDENTS, MISHAPS, AND BOORISH BEHAVIOR

There may be nothing more gracious than the host who thoughtfully reassures a guest who accidentally spills or breaks something. When a guest accidentally breaks a plate or a glass, however, it is up to him to offer to pay to replace it. While the guest's manners are obviously lacking if he doesn't at least offer, it is never correct for the host to remind him of his responsibility—even if what was lost was expensive or irreplaceable. Accidents do happen, and breakage is the cost of entertaining a large group of people.

If, on the other hand, a guest breaks something and insists on paying for it, but you feel uncomfortable billing him for the replacement, do and say nothing. If he persists, then you are perfectly correct in giving him an estimate on the cost.

If you are a guest at a party and accidentally break something, try to get an estimate of the item from your host. If he refuses, send him a check with a note of apology. Or try to find a replacement just like the one that was broken, especially if it is part of a set.

Some homeowners' insurance policies cover breakage in another's home. It is wise to check your policy before you buy a replacement; you just might be reimbursed.

INEBRIATED GUESTS

When someone has obviously had too much to drink at your party, it can be embarrassing for all concerned. Even more importantly, never let anyone who has had too much to drink get behind the wheel of a car. If there is no one to do the driving for him, see that a mutual friend takes him home safely, call a taxi, or put him to bed in your home. Your guest's car keys should be gently taken away if he refuses to go with someone else. This is for the safety of other travelers as well as your guest. Another important issue is the growing trend of finding a host or hostess legally liable if injury comes to the drinker or someone else.

If, on the other hand, *you* are the overimbibing offender who disrupted the party, you must recognize that your behavior was insulting or rude—and you should apologize immediately.

ETHNIC SLURS AND OFFENSIVE JOKES

If you find yourself in a social situation with people who make their prejudices known with ethnic slurs, you can do one of a number of things. If you find another's opinion totally unacceptable, try to change the subject as soon as possible. If that doesn't work, excuse yourself from the conversation, particularly if you care intensely about the subject and might become emotional in your response.

If you belong to the group under attack, you have

two choices. You can simply ignore it and avoid those people in the future. Or, you can bluntly say: "You must be talking about me. I'm Irish [or whatever it is]." Their shocked embarrassment can be almost as rewarding as their limp efforts to make amends; one can only hope this will temper their prejudice in the future. If there are people of the targeted group with you or in hearing range, your situation is more embarrassing. Try to change the conversation if you can. If you cannot, avoid the urge to rise to the defense, which might evoke an onslaught even more embarrassing to your friends. Keep your silence, break away when possible, and assure your friends of your support.

If you find yourself in a social gathering with a person who makes offensive jokes, you should feel no need to laugh or support such a display of poor taste. If you are the host, you need only interrupt him in the middle of the joke to ask for his help in another room. You can take him aside and tell him you think he has a wonderful sense of humor, but that he may be embarrassing the other guests by telling off-color jokes. If you are a guest who is offended by what another guest is saying, you may quietly say, "I don't appreciate that kind of remark." If the offensive slurs continue, turn your back or simply take your leave.

DROP-INS AND UNEXPECTED VISITS

Visits to friends, acquaintances, and even relative strangers range from spontaneous, informal drop-in visits to formal calls, with their own protocol and etiquette. The only etiquette involved in casual visits between close friends is that each be considerate of the other and never abuse the special bond of their friendship.

There is always the occasional relative, friend, or neighbor who thinks nothing of walking right in without knocking. If it bothers you, I say: lock your doors. While an occasional unannounced drop-in works out well—especially if it is immediate family or a close friend—more often it is inconvenient to the one visited. If you are the one doing the visiting, make sure to call beforehand.

If by chance you are just about to start your dinner when friends drop in, the polite response is to try to make the meal stretch to include them. If the meal cannot possibly feed an extra person or two, explain that you were about to eat and ask if they could stop by later.

As in most other situations, there are exceptions. Casual drop-ins at Christmas and Thanksgiving are common in many parts of the country, when visitors bearing good cheer tend to be more the norm. Even then, it's a good idea to call first before you drop by.

Chapter 19

WORKING WITH CATERERS

TIPS ON USING A CATERER

If you are planning an intimate cocktail party or a small wedding reception and have the help of family and friends, you probably don't need professional help in preparing and serving food and beverages. By preparing food in advance and freezing it, and by keeping the menu and the decorations as simple as possible, your party can be both inexpensive and, within reason, easy to manage.

Planning a larger party or reception in your home or anywhere else that provides no services, however, can be a lot of work. Entertaining a large group of guests with any degree of pleasure and relaxation may call for the aid of professional catering services or temporary help. Caterers let you be a guest at your own party.

The rule of thumb: Hiring a caterer or other temporary help is recommended for a party or reception of more than thirty guests. Depending on the size of the catering company, they can provide just the food or the works: food, beverages, a complete serving staff, crystal and china, tables, chairs, and linens; some even provide tents, dance floors, and party decorations—or can recommend reliable suppliers and vendors.

Caterers generally set prices based on a per-person figure. That figure varies from region to region, state to state, urban area to rural area. Costs are dependent on other factors as well: the formality of the occasion, the time of day, day of the week, the number of guests, what kind of food service you choose, how you choose to serve alcohol and other beverages, and the number of service people needed for the job.

Costs can run from twenty-five dollars per person for a beach clambake to six hundred dollars per person for a grand sit-down dinner in a major city. Having an open bar can add more than ten dollars per person to the total cost.

Don't forget to figure gratuities and taxes into your total costs; they can add up to 25 percent of the total bill.

TIPS ON WORKING WITH CATERERS:

GET A REFERRAL. Ask for names of recommended caterers from friends or coworkers. If you attend a party where the catering is outstanding, get the caterer's card for future reference.

BE SURE TO LOOK OVER THE CATERER'S PORTFOLIO. This is generally an album containing photographs of previous receptions. Look for creative touches: fruits and vegetables skillfully cut into beautiful shapes or arranged in eye-catching ways; interesting and complementary color schemes; a variety of dishes; and well-organized and attractive presentations, if you're considering a buffet. In other words, the food should be pretty enough to stand on its own.

SET UP A FOOD TASTING WITH CATERERS YOU ARE INTERVIEWING. Most caterers will be happy to do so. Ask for a variety of dishes, from hors d'ouevres to a main course to a dessert.

GET IT IN WRITING. Make sure that everything you need done is detailed in the catering contract and is matched by a price. There is nothing worse than finding out after the fact that a service you assumed would be included in the overall bill is in fact an extra cost.

FIND OUT WHAT IS INCLUDED. Does the caterer design centerpieces and, if so, does he offer choices? Does the caterer provide china, silverware, and glasses? Are gratuities included in the total price? What are overtime costs?

STICK TO YOUR BUDGET. Don't be seduced into buying unnecessary services that you can do yourself.

CATERER CHECKLIST

Once you and your caterer have agreed on arrangements, be absolutely sure that every service to be provided, and the total itemized costs, are given to you in a contract. Everything down to the last canapé must be specified. Specifically, the following points should be covered:

- Detailed menu and how it will be served.
- Beverages: open bar, champagne, soft drinks and other nonalcoholic beverages
- Number of serving staff total, and how many per table for a sit-down reception.
- Whether gratuities are included.
- Number and set-up of tables and chairs.
- Delivery charges.
- Deadline for guest count.
- Overtime charges.
- Tents or marquees.
- Whether glass and china are insured against breakage.
- Whether taxes are included in the estimate.
- Flowers and decorations (and coordination with florist).
- Table linen choices.
- Whether coat check and valet parking staff are provided or not.
- Meals for band, DJ, photographers, videographers.
- Additional fees for the rental of linens, china, flatware.
- Additional fees for set-up and clean-up.
- Form of last payment (check, credit card, certified check).
- Surcharges for heat or air conditioning.

CHAPTER 20

TIPS ON TOASTS

At a dinner party, it is the host or hostess' prerogative to offer the first toast. If none is offered, a guest may propose a toast to the hosts. If one of the hosts has given the first toast, a guest may propose a second one.

At informal dinners anyone may propose a toast as soon as wine or champagne is served.

Toasters need not drain their glasses. A small sip each time allows one to drink numerous toasts from one serving.

You don't have to have an alcoholic beverage to make a toast; you can use whatever liquid is available. Whether you drink or not, you should raise your water goblet or glass of soda and join in the spirit. It is extremely discourteous to remain seated.

The person being toasted does not rise or drink the toast. Instead the honoree rises and drinks to his or her toasters in return, either saying, "Thank you," or proposing his own toast to them. Or, the reply to a toast may simply be a smile and a nod in the direction of the speaker or a raise of the glass toward the speaker in a gesture of "Thanks, and here's to you, too," after the toast has been completed.

SAMPLE TOASTS

The following toasts are intended to give you some ideas for various occasions. They provide a framework in which to express your own feelings.

TOAST TO A RETIRING EMPLOYEE OR A MEMBER OF THE FIRM

"It is often said that nobody is indispensable, and that may sometimes be true. But for all of us there will never be anyone who can replace Joe. Although we will miss him greatly, we know how much he is looking forward to his retirement, and we wish him all the happiness he so richly deserves in the years to come."

TOAST TO A GUEST OF HONOR AT A TESTIMONIAL DINNER

"We are gathered here tonight to honor a woman who has given unselfishly of her time and effort to make this campaign so successful. Without the enthusiasm and leadership that Jane Doe has shown all through these past months, we could never have reached our goal. Please join me in drinking a toast to the woman who, more than anyone else, is responsible for making it possible to see our dream of a new hospital wing finally come true."

ENGAGEMENT-PARTY TOAST

This is the conventional announcement made by the father of the bride-to-be at a party or dinner in celebration of the engagement of his daughter. After seeing that all glasses at the table are filled, the host rises, lifts his own glass, and says, "I propose we drink to the health of Mary and the man she has decided to add to our family. I would like to propose a toast to them both, wishing them a lifetime of happiness."

Everyone except the future bride and groom rises and drinks a little of whatever the beverage may be. The bride or the groom may stand and make a few remarks thanking the guests for their good wishes, expressing happiness with each other and with each other's new families.

WEDDING-CELEBRATION TOASTS

Amend these toasts to fit the occasion when you are given the honor of making a toast at a wedding celebration, whether the rehearsal dinner or the reception.

A Bride or Bridegroom's Father's Toast at the Rehearsal Dinner.

"I would like to ask you to join me in drinking a toast to two wonderful people without whom this wedding could never have been possible: Veronica's mother and father, Mr. and Mrs. Brown."

And: *"I don't need to tell you what a wonderful person Lynn is, but I do want to tell you how happy Brett's mother and I are to welcome her as our new daughter-in-law. To Lynn and Brett."*

A Best Man's Toast to the Bridal Couple at the Wedding Reception.
"To Mary and John—may they always be as happy as they are today."

A Bridegroom's Toast to His Bride at the Wedding Reception.
"I'd like you all to join me in a toast to the woman who's just made me the happiest man in the world."

A Bride's and Bridegroom's Toast to Their Parents and Guests.
"We would like you to join us in a toast to our wonderful parents who helped make this day possible . . . and now we toast all of you, our family and friends, with thanks for helping make this such a special time for us."

ANNIVERSARY TOAST

"Many of us who are here tonight can well remember that day twenty-five years ago when we drank a toast to the future happiness of Ann and Roger. It is more than obvious that our good wishes at that time have served them well, and therefore I would like to ask that all of

you—old friends and new—rise and drink with me to another twenty-five years of the same love and happiness that Ann and Roger have already shared together."

TOASTS FOR ALL OCCASIONS

This is a toast that can be added to the end of a few personal words or said on its own. It is one that has sent myriad travelers on their way, blessed countless couples, events, and special people and warmed the hearts of all present:

> *May you*
> *have warm words*
> *on a cold evening,*
> *A full moon*
> *on a dark night,*
> *And the road*
> *downhill*
> *all the way*
> *to your door.*

TOASTS IN OTHER LANGUAGES

Since the custom of toasting originated in Europe and is still more widely practiced there than here, well-traveled Americans are bringing home toasts from abroad. A knowledge of the most common of these can be very useful, but if you are not sure of the pronunciation, use the equivalent English toast instead. The following examples all mean, translated, "To your health."

French: *À votre santé*.

Spanish: *Salud*.

German: *Prosit*.

Swedish: *Skål*.
(This is often taken to mean that the toasters must empty their glasses, but that is not necessary in the United States.)

Yiddish: *L'Chayim*.

Irish: *Slàinte*.

Italian: *Salute*.

Russian: *Na zdorovie*.

Polish: *Na zdrowie*.

INDEX